Women of the Bible
Volume 2

Faithful & Fruitful

by

Shirley M. Starr

ISBN   0-9728162-2-4

First Printing   September, 2003

NOTE: All Bible references taken from
the Authorized Version (KJV).

Printed in the U.S.A. by
Morris Publishing
3212 East Highway 30
Kearney, NE 68847
1-800-650-7888

Dedication

This book is dedicated
to my mother, **Betty Jane Zehr,** and
to my mother-in-law, **Ada Virginia Starr**.
Their faithful and fruitful Christian living
has inspired and motivated me.

♥ Thank you both for your godly example. ♥

Preface

The Bible discusses faithfulness and fruitfulness throughout its many holy pages. Several ladies in the Scriptures depict this in their own personal walks with the Lord. Some of these ladies lived in Old Testament times of war, poverty, and strife. Others personally worked alongside Jesus, Peter, and the Apostle Paul in their early ministries, facing illness, danger, and persecution.

Whatever the setting in their personal lives, these ladies remained faithful to and fruitful for their Lord and Master, Jesus Christ. Their circumstances did not hinder them from producing fruit. Their fruit remains embedded in the Scriptures as golden nuggets to be remembered and treasured by ladies of today.

May this volume of Bible women encourage you, dear sister, to remain faithful and fruitful wherever you are in your own walk with the Lord.

> 'Blessed is the man that trusteth in the Lord, and whose hope the Lord is. For he shall be like a tree planted by the waters, and that spreadeth out her roots by the river, and shall not see, when heat cometh, but her leaf shall be green; and shall not be careful in the year of drought, **neither shall cease from yielding fruit.**' *(Jeremiah 17:7-8)*

> 'Ye have not chosen me, but I have chosen you, and ordained you, that ye should **go and bring forth fruit**, and that your fruit should remain: that whatsoever ye shall ask of the Father in my name, he may give it you.' *(John 15:16)*

Table of Contents
Women of the Bible, Volume 2
Faithful & Fruitful

Title page
Copyright page
Dedication page
Preface

Sources
How to Order additional copies

Chapter 1

RAHAB

The Prostitute
"From Harlotry to Sainthood"

Facts

Husband:	Salmon
Children:	Boaz
Occupation:	Prostitute
Her name means:	"broad, wide, insolence, spaciousness"

Her Home and Occupation (Josh. 2:1,13; Matt. 1:5; Heb. 11:31)

Rahab, also known as Rachab in Matthew 1:5, lived during the conquest of Canaan when Joshua led the Israelites. She lived in Jericho, the "most important city of the Jordan valley." *(New Ungers, p. 671)* This city was crucial to the Israelites as it was so well fortified and near the passes into the western mountains.

Rahab had her own home facing the outer wall of the city. The walls of Jericho were two feet thick with a twelve to fifteen foot gap in between. Houses were built over this gap. Because of the location of her home, it would have been the only one to which strangers had access.

According to Joshua 2:13, Rahab had a mother and brothers and sisters, though none of their names are given. Because she was a harlot, we find the Scriptures using this term repetitively, perhaps to show us God's grace in her life. Jewish writers did not interpret her as a harlot because they disliked the association, so they called her a "hostess." She also may have manufactured flax and dyed it.

1

She appeared to be high-spirited and independent. Perhaps her family had kicked her out of their home due to her wicked lifestyle.

Joshua knew the importance of taking this city for his people. God had given him specific instructions to conquer the land, so he sent spies out to canvass the land.

Her Courage (Josh. 2:2-8; Rom. 3:7-8; Heb. 13:2)

The spies took refuge in Rahab's house since it was nearest the outer wall. Since she was a harlot, no one would think it odd to see strangers enter her house. Note God's providence in this! By befriending these strangers, she actually lived out Hebrews 13:2 which says, "Be not forgetful to entertain strangers: for thereby some have entertained angels unawares."

The king of Jericho heard of their arrival and sent messengers asking Rahab to deliver the men into their hands. Rahab had hidden the spies on her roof covering them with stalks of flax. She lied to the messengers and told them the men had left at dark. The Bible does not commend her lying, but commends her faith. Remember, at this time, she was not a believer. Matthew Henry wrote, "God accepted her faith and pardoned her infirmity." She had heard reports of these Israelites and how they were conquering the land. Maybe her faith had been sparked, and she desired to hear and know more. Whatever the case, she showed great creativity in hiding them.

By hiding the spies, she turned against her own countrymen to turn toward God, even though treason was punishable by death. We will see this principle of separation throughout the whole account of Rahab. She risked her own life to save others! What courage she had!

Her Faith (Josh. 2:9-11; Heb. 11:31)

Rahab had heard reports of God's power forty years ago! She says in Joshua 2:9-10,

> " . . . I know that the LORD hath given you the land, and that your terror is fallen upon us, and that all the inhabitants of the land faint because of you. For we have heard how the LORD dried up the water of the Red sea for you, when ye came out of Egypt; and what ye did unto the two kings of the Amorites . . . whom ye utterly destroyed."

She knew God had given them the land and encouraged them by informing them the enemy was afraid of **them**! How do we know this? She used the words "terror" and "faint." She went on to tell them in verse 11 that her countrymen's "hearts did melt, neither did there remain any more courage in any man, because of you . . ." The Israelites were a legend in the land because of what God had done for them. Everyone knew of their great victories.

Rahab's faith in Israel's God was greater than her fear of men. She demonstrated a healthy fear of the Lord and admitted His sovereignty as she confessed in verse 11: " . . . for the LORD your God, he is God in heaven above, and in earth beneath." By saying this, she demonstrated her belief in God. Do you have a healthy fear of the Lord? Are you quick to tell others of His wonderful works in your own life? Can others see by your life that He is the one and true God "in heaven above, and in earth beneath?"

Her faith was so great that she is one of the two women mentioned by name in the Hebrews "roll call of faith." *(Heb. 11:31)* The only other woman named is Sarah. What an honor this is for Rahab! "God took her tarnished portrait, cleansed it, and hung it next to Sarah in the gallery of the heroes of faith. These two women are the only two females in a long list of men." *(Karssen, Vol. 1, p. 75)* It is amazing that a harlot would be included in God's hall of faith! This shows us that there is no respect of persons with our Lord. It matters not what your past was. Jesus' precious blood washes all that sin away and puts you in Heaven's "roll call of faith!" Your name is written in the Lamb's book of life if you have confessed and believed like Rahab did.

Her Plan   (Ex. 12:13; Josh. 2:12-21; Heb. 9:22)

Rahab developed a plan. (Isn't it just like us women to have a plan?) She bargained with the spies. Since she was saving their nation, would they save her family? Being unselfish, she did not ask for wealth or fame. Instead, she became an intercessor for her family and asked the spies to swear to her that they would save her family and all that they had. Oh, that we as ladies would be intercessors for our families today! Are we concerned about their spiritual state? Do we hold them before the throne of the Lord in daily prayer? Do we pray even five minutes a day for our husbands, children, parents? May God make us intercessors for our generation!

The spies promised to save her if she kept the deal a secret. Because she had shown mercy, they would show her mercy. Matthew Henry said, "Those that show mercy may expect to find mercy."

Agreeing to the matter, she immediately put action to her faith and helped them to escape. Who does this remind us of? Jochebed acted in a similar manner when she made the basket for baby Moses (and is mentioned unnamed in Hebrews 11:23).

There was a progression to Rahab's faith. She **heard** that "God had given them the land," *(Josh. 2:9)*, she **believed** that "he is God in heaven above and in earth beneath," *(Josh. 2:11)*, and she **acted** on her belief by letting them down "by a cord through the window." *(Josh. 2:15)* James 2:25-26 commends Rahab even more for her faith. "Likewise also, was not Rahab the harlot justified by works, when she had received the messengers, and had sent them out another way? For as the body without the spirit is dead, so faith without works is dead also."

There were three provisions to her plan:

1. Rahab was to hang a scarlet cord in the window. The same cord she used to preserve them would later save her and her family, as she was to place it in the window when the spies returned. *(Joshua 2:18)* The scarlet cord was a symbol of the blood upon the doorpost in Exodus 12:13 and a symbol of the blood of Jesus Christ in Hebrews 9:22. **Salvation through the blood!**
2. Her family was to be in her house. How else would the Israelites distinguish her family from anyone else? We see this same principle in Noah's family. Everyone had to be out of the world and in the ark. Lot was also told to get his family out of Sodom. **Separation!**
3. She was to keep the deal a secret. *(Josh. 2:20)* **Commitment!**

Are you saved, separated, and committed? Maybe you have taken the step of salvation, but have not progressed in your walk with the Lord. Meditate on Rahab's faith and her walk. Use her as a pattern for your own walk with the Lord.

Her Salvation   (Josh. 2:21-24, 6:17, 22-23,25; Acts 16:31)

After hiding for three days in the mountains, the spies took back a good report because of Rahab. How wisely she used her power of influence! Do people give a good report of you because of your wisdom and walk with the Lord, or are you always negative, causing others to give a bad report? Our power of influence stretches widely among our family and friends. We must use it wisely for the Lord.

Imagine Rahab's feelings as the Israelites were marching around Jericho! Was there some fear and trepidation? After the seventh trip around the city, the walls fell flat—all but hers! She and her entire family were saved! God's timing was perfect! The Bible says the spies "brought out all her kindred." *(Josh. 6:23)* She had influenced them **all** for the Lord and convinced them to come to her home. What a testimony in contrast to Lot who failed to protect his family!

She was left for a while "without the camp of Israel." Why? This shows her uncleanness. Unclean people had to stay outside the camp for a certain number of days. There were probably some complaining Israelites who asked what right she had to be among them! Though they had just experienced a great victory because of her, perhaps they looked on her as a foreigner not measuring up to their standards and not good enough for them. Are we guilty of this same attitude today when others come into our assembly to worship? Do we reach out to that visitor and make her feel wanted and included like Jesus would? Remember, this converted harlot was listed by name in the hall of faith. *(Heb. 11)*

Little did Rahab know what great joy awaited her in serving the Lord, and what a wise decision she had made by professing her belief in the God of Israel!

Her Later Life (Matt. 1:5)

Not only was Rahab mentioned in God's great hall of faith, but she is also listed in the genealogy of Jesus Christ. (Tamar and Bathsheba were other women with shameful pasts included in the line of Christ.) Rahab was converted to Judaism and married into a leading family of Israel. She married a man named Salmon who, some conjecture, could have been one of the spies. Her little boy's name was Boaz. She became the great-great grandmother of David and, therefore, an ancestress of Jesus Christ. She is known as Rachab in Matthew 1:5.

This happy ending to a bad beginning shows us the extension of God's love and mercy. Surely, our God "is able also to save them to the uttermost that come unto God by him . . ." *(Heb. 7:25)* Rahab became a woman of faith and works. Can the same be said of us?

Conclusions

(1 Sam. 2:30; Psa. 87:4; 89:10; Isa. 51:9; Matt. 21:31-32; Acts 10:34-35)

Rahab's story shows us God's purging power. His blood makes the vilest sinner clean, and He is not limited by the depth of our darkness. Some of the greatest Bible heroes we know rose from debauched failure and became godly people, including Paul, Zaccheus, and Mary Magdalene.

God did not wait until Rahab was perfect to use her. He waited only for her to demonstrate that spark of faith. It matters not what Rahab had been, but rather what she became. Are you dwelling on the dark things of the past? Has Satan convinced you that you are not good enough for God to use? Remember, God still used Rahab even though her life had been blemished.

Rahab did not let her past sin mar her present service for the Lord. Her past reputation did not deter her from pursuing her present relationship with Him. She was confident that He, Who had begun a good work in her, would perform it until the day of Jesus Christ. *(Phil. 1:6)*

The Apostle Paul faced this difficult struggle in his own life due to his own reprehensible past. He testified in Philippians 3:13: ". . .but this one thing I do, forgetting those things which are behind, and reaching forth unto those things which are before."

Satan takes great delight in heaping false guilt upon us concerning the past. He loves to make us feel we are "no good" and of no use to the Lord. Paul instructed believers in Romans 8:1: "There is therefore now no condemnation to them which are in Christ Jesus, who walk not after the flesh but after the Spirit."

God forgets our past when we repent and accept His blood sacrifice for our sins. "As far as the east is from the west, so far hath he removed our transgressions from us." *(Psa. 103:12)*

"Maybe you are like Rahab in the sense that you are aching on the inside because of a hapless past, a critical present, and a bleak future, but no one would ever guess because of the outside "front" you've managed to put on." *(Briscoe, p. 46)* If you have accepted Christ's scarlet thread of sacrifice in your life, you are **somebody** to Him. You are a daughter of the King of Kings!

Don't allow Satan to plague you with false guilt, doubts, and fears! Don't be double-minded in your service for the Lord! Become single-minded like Rahab, and let your faith produce good works. Refuse to allow Satan to "beat you down" and keep you paralyzed in your service for God. Reach forth for those things which are before, and "whatsoever thy hand findeth to do, do it with thy might . . ." *(Eccl. 9:10)* Be a modern day Rahab!

Rahab's story pictures Christ reaching out to the Gentiles. We see her name linked with symbolism speaking of Egypt in Psalms 84 and 87. She believed, confessed with her mouth, and acted on her faith. She was concerned about the salvation of others. The spies coming to her home was no accident but was really the providence of God. Who knows what God may have for you to do?

Rahab's Roles

1. Wife
2. Mother
3. Harlot
4. Liar
5. Intercessor
6. Soul-winner
7. Traitor
8. Encourager

Rahab's Character Traits

1. Ambition
2. Independence
3. High-spiritedness
4. Boldness
5. Courage
6. Cleverness
7. Alertness
8. Unselfishness
9. Devotion

Chapter 2

JAEL
The Traitor

Facts

Husband:	Heber
Children:	None known
Occupation:	Housewife
Her name means:	"wild goat," "gazelle"

Her Heritage

(Judg. 1:16; 2:13-19; 3:3-4; 4:11, 16-17; 5:24)

The great leader, Joshua, had died, and the Israelites continued in their backslidden ways of serving Baalim. The book of Judges tells us God delivered them over to "spoilers . . . and sold them into the hands of their enemies round about . . ." *(Judg. 2:14)* Nevertheless, because of His great and undying compassion for His people, He provided judges who delivered them from their enemies. However, the Israelites would not learn or hearken, and when the judge died, they would once again return to their sin. So, the Lord allowed the Philistines, the Canaanites, the Sidonians, and the Hivites to prove His people by threatening war. Israel would then cry out to God for help.

During this time God raised up two great leaders, Deborah and Barak, who defeated the Canaanites and their leader, the great captain Sisera, who had 900 chariots of iron.

It was just after this that our heroine, Jael, came on the scene. Her tribe, the Kenites, came from the mountains and were nomads. They were also thought to have been metalsmiths and may even have helped to make Sisera's 900 chariots. She was married to Heber, the Kenite. The Kenites were relatives of

Moses' father-in-law. *(Judg. 1:16, 4:11)* They were a tribe of Canaan whose country had been given to Abraham. *(Nave, p. 773)*

The amazing thing about this story is that there had always been peace between the King of Hazor and Heber. So, after the battle, Sisera fled on foot to the tent of Heber and Jael, thinking he would be safe there. Why would he go to a tent for safety?

1. Perhaps there would be less **suspicion**. Jael was just a housewife—a woman in the tent. Who would look for him there? *(Judg. 5:24)*
2. Perhaps it was the nearest **site** and a good location for him.
3. Perhaps he thought there was **security** there, as he would be among friends.

Little did he know what kind of hospitality awaited him!

Her Hospitality   (Judg. 4:18-20)

In Bible days, there was a "code of hospitality" of which Jael probably was well aware. This code involved five different things:

1. The guest was always invited in. *(Judg. 4:18)*
2. No questions were asked.
3. He was provided with water to wash his feet and given food.
4. He was offered protection by the host. (Remember Lot and his guests?)
5. The guest never left alone or empty-handed.

Hospitality was considered right and honorable. Any infraction was considered an outrage.

How does this compare with our hospitality of today? Don't we usually ask our guests in and provide refreshment for them? We protect them while they are in our home and often send gifts of food with them. In Romans 12:13, Paul instructs the believers to be "given to hospitality," and "distributing to the necessity of saints." Pastors and deacons are to open their homes to others and be "given to hospitality" also. *(1 Tim. 3:2, Titus 1:8)* We see hospitality demonstrated over and over again in the Bible. What a ministry hospitality is! How are you doing with this ministry?

Jael started out right with her hospitality, but did not keep the whole code of hospitality. We see her at the tent door, opening the flap, and inviting Sisera in, calling him Lord and telling him not to fear. She gave him a feeling of security and safety as her guest. He asked her for a little water to drink, and she gave him milk and even covered him up. Warm milk is known to help one sleep. Did she know that and warm the milk first? What were her motives in her hospitality?

Her Hostility (Judg. 4:20-21; 5:26)

Jael broke the hospitality code. Sisera instructed her to stand in the door of the tent and lie and tell anyone who came by that she had not seen him. We do not see Jael agreeing to do this. After Sisera dozed off and was in a deep sleep, we see Jael's hospitality turning to hostility. She took a tent peg (nail) and a hammer and softly approached Sisera. She drove the nail right through his temple. Matthew Henry said, "He that thought to destroy Israel with his many iron chariots is himself destroyed with one iron nail." She was evidently used to swinging a hammer, as women made the tents, pitched them, and took care of them. As if that were not enough, she proceeded to cut off his head! What kind of hospitality was this? Why did she do it? What were her motives?

1. **Selfishness?** Was she looking out for her own skin?
2. **Fear?** She was **not** an Israelite and may have feared vengeance for sheltering Sisera.

3. **Patriotism?** She knew the Israelites had the "upper
hand," and by killing Sisera saved her own
people from being plundered.

Whatever the case, she lied, committed treachery, and
murdered. Did she get ahead of God and not allow Him to
execute divine punishment, or was she an instrument used of
God? Though it was indeed a treacherous act, she demonstrated
resourcefulness and used what was available at the time.

Though Sisera thought he had all under control, and his life
would be spared, God knew differently. "God often brings ruin
on His enemies when they are most elevated." *(Matthew Henry)*

Her Heroism   (Judg. 4:9; 5:24-27)

Anyone who killed the enemy would have been Israel's hero
or heroine. Although Jael committed a dastardly deed, God
commended her as a heroine in Deborah's song in Judges 5:24.
She is called "blessed above women." Deborah was probably
praising Jael's faith and not her treachery. This was a similar
situation to that of Rahab when she hid the spies and had faith in
the Israelites' God. Jael fulfilled Deborah's prophecy in Judges
4:9 when she said, "the Lord shall sell Sisera into the hand of a
woman."

Conclusions   (Judg. 5:28-30; 9:53-54)

Jael showed how brave and courageous a woman can be, or
how cruel and hard-hearted a woman can be. She committed a
crime in the name of patriotism. What does a woman do when at
war and her people are in danger? Did Jael learn a spark of faith
from Moses' father-in-law who had been a godly man and
recognized and claimed God's goodness to Moses? *(Ex. 18:9-
12)* Perhaps she had come to believe on the Israelites' God just
like Rahab. She "only acted a part that accomplished an

important purpose of heaven." Once again God used a weak thing to confound the wise, a tent peg not a mighty iron chariot.

Are there things in your life that you think are too weak for the Lord to use? Do you think you have nothing to offer the Lord? You need only be available and use the resources you have for the Lord. Perhaps God is only asking you to take the next step of obedience in your Christian walk, or maybe you are hiding a talent under a bushel. Remember, God said, "thou hast been faithful over a few things, I will make thee ruler over many things. . ." *(Matt. 25:21)*

Sisera's mother waited for him to come home from the battle. What was taking him so long? She and her attendants showed how wicked the people were. Even the women accepted the fact that soldiers would abuse the enemy's women. All they were concerned about were the material things, which would be brought home to them! *(Judg. 5:30)* How sad! They were caught up in the worship of things.

How about you? What are your goals in life? To give so you can get? To climb the ladder of success regardless of others and their feelings? To make it to the top? It is often a lonely position at the top, especially when you have trampled over your friends to get there. Are you so caught up in things that you keep your family in constant debt by compulsive spending? Have your priorities become mixed up like those of Sisera's mother and her court? It is not too late to re-prioritize and put the Lord and His work first in your life.

Authors differ in their interpretation of this Biblical event. Some deeply criticize Jael and her deed while others praise her and say she was an instrument used of God. Whatever the case, she delivered God's people from tyranny and is praised for it in Deborah's song. It was a disgrace to die at the hand of a woman, and Sisera's shame became Jael's glory. The Israelites had rest for forty years after this wartime event. "Jael's treachery was forgotten in the more important fact of her courage." *(Lockyer, p. 70)*

Jael's Roles

1. Housewife
2. Patriot
3. Traitor
4. Murderer
5. Liar

Jael's Character Traits

1. Courage
2. Resourcefulness
3. Decisiveness
4. Hospitality
5. Hostility

Chapter 3

RUTH

The Young Widow
Romance and Redemption
"From Rags to Riches"

Facts	
Husband:	Mahlon, Boaz
Children:	Obed
Occupation:	Housewife, Gleaner
Her name means	Beauty, friendship, a female friend, a sight, something worth seeing

Background   (Judges 2:11-23; 21:25)

Ruth is a love story of redemption, a story "set against the dark background of the apostasy and foreign oppression of the period of the judges." *(Ryrie, p. 406)* It is a story of "a little foreign girl who came out of paganism and idolatry." *(McGee, Vol. 2, p. 88)*

The book of Ruth tells us about a family that was falling apart, about God's judgment on that family, about a woman who became bitter, and finally about how God rescued this family and put their lives back together.

The story takes place during the time of the judges, when there was no king - a time of anarchy and apathy. The Bible tells us that everyone did what was right in his own eyes. Sandwiched in the middle of this crisis, God give us the beautiful love story of Boaz and Ruth.

Walking Out of God's Will <small>(Gen. 19:36-37; Num. 25:1-2; Ruth 1:1-5; 1 Kings 11:1)</small>

The story begins in Bethlehem-judah during a turbulent time of famine. The irony of the story is that "Bethlehem" means "house of bread," and "Judah" means "praise." However, it was a time of severe hardship and great hunger. Elimelech decided to take his wife and sons and go to a foreign country to obtain food. Gathering his wife, Naomi, and their sons, Mahlon and Chilion, he set off for the heathen country of Moab. It seemed that Elimelech did not trust God to take care of his family. We do not see him seeking God about going. On the other hand, he probably hated to see their hunger and took it upon himself as the breadwinner to supply in some manner.

He was up against a brick wall, but did not allow his extremity to become God's opportunity. His first mistake was trying to run away from his problems. He feared death due to the famine. That which they all feared came upon them. *(Job 3:25)* Once this family began making mistakes, it was as if they were on a treadmill and could not get off.

Moab was a heathen country whose name meant "washpot." These people were descendants from the incest of Lot with his oldest daughter. They were an outcast people wholly involved in idolatry. *(Num. 25:1-2)* The Moabite women were called "strange women" in 1 Kings 11:1 and had seduced the Israelite men who promptly became unequally yoked in marriage to them, strictly forbidden by God.

Why would anyone want to move to Moab? Why would anyone want that type of influence for his family? Like Lot, Elimelech's family became a prodigal family and was to experience much sorrow in this foreign country. After entering this country, we are told in Ruth 1:2 that the family "continued there." Perhaps they were not willing to abandon their standard of living. They did not just go to obtain food supplies and then return to Bethlehem. They stayed and possibly began to incorporate some of the heathen ways.

How important it is to seek the Lord before any major move. We will see through this story how sometimes it is unwise to move for money or promotion. Is there a good Bible-believing church in the area – a place where your family can grow and serve the Lord? Often the "grass looks greener on the other side," and we need to remain patient and wait upon the Lord. Often we "get what we want, but lose what we had." The Psalmist verified this in Psalm 106:15 when he wrote, "And he gave them their request; but sent leanness into their soul." Beware of becoming lean in your soul!

We see that the "Elimelech family" looked at their problem only from a human standpoint. From their perspective, all they could see in Bethlehem was hunger and death. All they could see in Moab was plenty to eat. Jesus said in Matthew 4:4, "But he answered and said, It is written, Man shall not live by bread alone, but by every word that proceedeth out of the mouth of God." From God's viewpoint, Moab was a heathen land of false gods and enemies to Him and Israel.

They also looked at their problem from the physical and emotional standpoint, not the spiritual. For them, the problem was a lack of food and a fear of the future. What is it for us? Shelter, money, security, companionship, sex, fame, protection? Remember that Jesus' first temptation was a choice between the physical and the spiritual. Life did not turn out the way they all expected.

Scripture tells us that Elimelech died, and Naomi was left with her two sons. They, like the other Israelite men, took wives "from the women of Moab." Mahlon married Ruth and Chilion married Orpah.

The sorrow increased for Naomi as both of her sons died and after ten years she was left alone with her daughters-in-law. What would she do? Where would she go? How would she earn a living? Now there were three widows with no male support.

Were Mahlon's and Chilion's lives shortened due to their disobedience of taking "strange women" as wives?

Widowhood and Poverty (Ruth 1:6-22)

Imagine Naomi's feelings! She heard there was now food back in Bethlehem and longed for her old country and friends. It was depressing to be a widow in a strange land. Unlike Lot's wife, she did not want to remain in the foreign country any longer. There was no reason to remain.

Encouraging her daughters-in-law to stay and find husbands, she made preparations to leave. She told Orpah and Ruth to return to their mothers' homes, and then she kissed them and cried and wept over them. She admitted that God was chastising her in Ruth 1:13 when she said, "the hand of the LORD is gone out against me." They were experiencing great grief and poverty. Notice that Naomi's chastisement not only affected her, but Orpah and Ruth also. So it is with us today. The consequences of our sin never just affect us. Naomi wanted them to count the cost of going with her because if they went with her they would experience what it was like to be a stranger in a foreign land.

Orpah kissed Naomi, but "Ruth clave unto her." Orpah had an affection for Naomi, but not enough to leave her own country. Isn't that just like some today? They have an affection for the Lord Jesus, but not enough to totally commit every area of their lives to Him.

Ruth, on the other hand, was unselfish, decisive, devoted, and contented (not complaining). We see her demonstrating no self-pity. Naomi encouraged her to return with Orpah. She knew first-hand what it would be like for Ruth to accompany her to Bethlehem. The customs and culture were entirely different. What an adjustment it would be for Ruth!

However, Ruth was not to be put off. It seems that she had accepted Naomi's Lord, as she made a seven-fold decision at this time. She said in Ruth 1:16-17:

1. "Whither thou goest, I will go." (She accepted her nation.)
2. "Where thou lodgest, I will lodge." (She accepted Naomi's poverty.)
3. "Thy people shall be my people." (She identified with God's people.)
4. "Thy God, my God." (She accepted Naomi's God.)
5. "Where thou diest, will I die."
6. "There will I be buried."
7. "If aught but death part thee and me." (Her decision was permanent.)

Ruth made a complete turn-around in the opposite direction. What do we call this? Repentance! By contrast, Orpah came, shed a few tears, but did not repent. Tears are **not** repentance! Notice that this did not happen until Naomi took steps in the right direction herself and returned from her backslidden state. What a testimony we are to others! Can others see Jesus in us? Are we pointing them in the right direction? If we would move toward Jesus, maybe others would follow.

The two ladies proceeded on their journey. According to Scripture, they returned to Bethlehem empty. The people of the town did not even recognize Naomi. The years of sorrow and grief had taken their toll on her. She admitted they had gone out full and returned empty. *(Ruth 1:21)* Likewise, she recognized the Lord's hand in it all when she said, "The LORD hath testified against me and the Almighty hath afflicted me." What an example and warning to us to remain in God's will and not to go against direct commands from His Word. J. Vernon McGee said, "When you go out from His presence and lose your fellowship you're going to find out that you get your whipping in the far country." *(McGee, p. 95)* The prodigal family had returned.

Working Woman

(Lev. 19:9-10, 23:22; Deut. 24:19; Ruth 2:1-23;
Psa. 37:23; 1 Tim. 5:11-13; Titus 2:5)

Immediately we see one of Ruth's good character traits surface. She and Naomi had returned at the time of barley harvest. Ruth asked Naomi if she could go to glean in the fields. She was willing to work showing her diligence and ambition. Gleaning in the fields for leftovers, a lowly job, was permitted to the poor and strangers. *(Lev. 19:9-10, 23:22, Deut. 24:19)* Up to thirty percent of the grain was left in the fields for the poor. This confirms the drastic straits they faced at the time.

Ruth began to live by her new faith. She learned God's Word and acted upon it. She knew about the gleaning law and was willing to work hard. She also looked out for Naomi and took care of her. God used the new convert, Ruth. Instead of remaining in depression and the doldrums, she took action. Demonstrating a submissive spirit, she sought Naomi's permission to glean. *(Ruth 2:2)*

God was totally in control of their situation as Christ's birth depended upon Ruth getting in the right field. Boaz was the most eligible bachelor in Bethlehem. He was wealthy and a kinsman of Naomi's. He "fell" for Ruth! Was it love at first sight? Treating her kindly and offering her protection, he went out of his way to invite her to glean. Again we see Ruth submit to the reapers and seek their permission to glean. *(Ruth 2:7)* Expressing a thankful and submissive heart, she bowed before Boaz. *(Ruth 2:10)*

Ruth was totally amazed and asked how she, a stranger, could find grace in his sight. What a beautiful example of our Lord's grace to us! Word of her good character had spread. Boaz said he knew of her kindness to Naomi and of her willingness to leave her country to go to a foreign land. She demonstrated the following traits:

1. **Loyalty** and a servant's heart to her mother-in-law.

2. **Courage** and bravery in leaving her own family.
3. **Faithfulness** – a keeper at home; not idle going from
    house to house. *(1 Tim. 5:11-13; Titus 2:5)*
4. **Trust in the Lord** – "under whose wings thou art come to
    trust." *(Ruth 2:11)*

Because of her gratefulness and submission, God worked on
her behalf. Boaz invited her to dinner, and he even ate with the
workers, showing a good employer-employee relationship! Of
course, he was motivated by Ruth's presence! What did they
have at this dinner?

1. They had bread, the usual food of servants.
2. They dipped it in vinegar. The poor used this to help them
    cool off.
3. They also had "corn nuts" or parched corn.

Boaz instructed his servants to treat Ruth kindly and let extra
grain fall for her. Naomi's faithfulness was finally being
rewarded. Ruth took home an ephah (about one-half bushel) of
barley, which was enough to last them five days. She had even
saved some of her lunch for Naomi and reported the whole day's
events to Naomi. Notice their good communication! Naomi told
Ruth that Boaz was a near kinsman. What a good relationship
they had!

In a day of deteriorating family relationships, here is a
wonderful example of what God would want for us! Often jokes
are made about mothers-in-law and daughters-in-law; however,
God would have this to be a beautiful and rewarding friendship.
Mothers-in-law need to accept their daughters-in-law just like
one of their own daughters and treat them on an equal basis.
Likewise, daughters-in-law should extend an arm of friendship
and acceptance to their "new mother."

Often a mother-in-law makes the mistake of wanting her
daughter-in-law to do everything her way, forgetting that she

came from a different family with different training. The mother-in-law mistakenly continues to serve her son instead of letting his new wife do that. She expects the "new daughter" to cook or keep house just like she does. The wife never feels like she can meet her mother-in-law's expectations. This serves to breed strife and contention. Evidently Naomi and Ruth did not face this situation or had weathered it together. They became close friends.

Mothers-in-law, if your "new daughter" lives nearby, find little ways to please her. What are some of her likes and dislikes? Occasionally bless her with a small gift. When she is weary with the care of little ones, make her a pot of soup or a dessert, helping to lighten her load. Offer to baby-sit and give her a couple of hours to herself. Do not infringe on her time. Compliment her. Go shopping with her once every month or so. Take her out to eat if you can.

Daughters-in-law, show appreciation to your "new mother." Do not take her for granted and always drop the kids off at her house. She has a life, too. Learn her favorite little things and once in a while bless her with a small item or a note of encouragement. Draw on her years of experience by asking her "how to" questions. Emulate Naomi and Ruth!

Relationship With Boaz   (Lev. 25:25-27, 47-51; Deut. 25:5-10; Ruth 3:1-18)

Naomi was a matchmaker and encouraged the relationship between Ruth and Boaz. She sought rest or security for Ruth in marriage. Since Boaz was a kinsman, there was certain protocol to follow. Naomi explained it and coached Ruth in the matter.

What was the job of the kinsman? *(Lev. 25:25-27, 47-51)*

1. To **marry** the widow and **redeem** the land. (This was usually done by the closest male relative.)
2. To **protect** the deceased and his inheritance.
3. To **redeem** from indebtedness.

The Levirate Law stated that when the husband died, the widow could call upon the nearest brother-in-law to be a husband. If there were no brother-in-law, then the nearest of kin was approached. *(Deut. 25:5-10)*

Notice God's concern for women here! He provided this law to help look out after the women and keep the land within the family. What a great life insurance program! In that system of law, it was Ruth's move to claim her husband!

Naomi planned the approach. *(Illustration from McGee, p. 108-109, Ruth 3:3-4.)*

1. **Wash thyself**	**Regeneration**
2. **Anoint thyself**	**Holy Spirit**
3. **Put thy raiment upon thee**	**Robe of righteousness**
4. **Get thee down to the floor**	**Claim Him as Redeemer**
5. **Uncover his feet**	**Worship Him**

Notice that Ruth had to make the first move. Boaz wanted to be her kinsman-redeemer, but she had to take the first step. Christ, wanting to be our Saviour, is waiting for us to take the first step!

Ruth had to go down to the threshing floor when everyone was asleep to begin this process. She was not being a "floozy" by doing this. This was the season of harvest when the families camped around the threshing floor, so there were many people present. After eating, the men would get in a circle with their heads pointed toward the grain to sleep. Thus, they protected the grain from thieves. *(McGee, p. 107)*

> Threshing floors are in danger of being robbed. For this reason someone always sleeps on the floor until the grain is removed. In Syria, at the threshing season, it is customary for the family to move out to the vicinity of the threshing-floor. A booth is constructed for shade; the mother prepares the meals and takes her turn with the father and children at riding on the sledge. *(Orr, Vol. v, p. 2976)*

Ruth explicitly obeyed Naomi's instructions. She realized her condition and went to the person who could do something about it. Do you realize your condition today, dear lady? The worst part of your life is not your money problems, your marriage problems, your job problems, or your family problems. The worst part is a spiritually bankrupt and backslidden condition. If you face that condition today, you need to go to the right Person.

Too often we look to the wrong people, run to the wrong places, and do the wrong things to solve our problems. Drinking will not help us! Drugs are not the answer! An affair is not the fix! Forsake all of those things and go to the Redeemer, the One who shed His precious blood. He can forgive, cleanse, and comfort! He can give wisdom and put your life back together like He did Ruth's. He is waiting for you to claim your possessions in Him.

We see Ruth doing just that. Being eager to claim her family possessions, she hurried down to the threshing floor. She waited until Boaz had finished eating and drinking. *(Ruth 3:3)* Why? Did Naomi know the way to a man's heart? Ruth lay at his feet and not at his side. Around midnight, Boaz awoke and was startled by the woman lying near his feet. He called out to see who it was. With great humility, Ruth answered, "Ruth, thine handmaid." She continued by asking him to spread his skirt over her. This was an Arabic custom as a token of marriage. It was a legal call, asking Boaz to take care of her.

Notice Boaz's three responses to her coming. He **accepted** her and blessed her in Ruth 3:10 -11. He promised that he would do all that she had requested. After accepting her, he **assured** her and told her not to fear. To seal this assurance, he gave her a down payment of six measures of barley. *(Ruth 3:15)* Finally, he **assisted** her. He went to the gate and finished the work. *(Ruth 3:18, 4:1)* What a wonderful picture this is of our Saviour! He **accepts** us just as we are by His finished work on the Cross! Then He **assures** us by giving us the earnest of the Holy Spirit.

Finally, He **assists** us by His intercession for us and His preparation of a place for us!

Boaz praised her for not seeking younger men. *(Ruth 3:10)* He wanted to protect her good reputation as a virtuous woman, so he asked her to wait until morning to leave. He also informed her that there was a nearer kinsman. By giving her a gift of grain, he assured Naomi of his care also. Naomi was pleased and realized that Boaz loved Ruth and would act quickly on the matter. It was his job to do the work of redemption. Ruth had taken the first step.

Have you taken that first step to Christ? Does the Holy Spirit speak to your heart during the invitation at church, but you keep putting it off? Are you waiting for a better time or another day? Christ, like Boaz, is waiting for you to claim your inheritance. However, He will not make you do it. He wants a willing heart, not a robot. Won't you yield to His call?

Rags to Riches   (Deut. 25:9; Ruth 4:1-22; Matt. 1:5)

Boaz did not wait to put the plan into action. Once Ruth claimed him as her kinsman-redeemer, he did everything properly and orderly. He sought out the nearest kinsman. He went to the gate, the place of business transactions (similar to our courthouse today). Using wisdom, he took ten witnesses with him. The kinsman just "happened" to walk by.

Boaz called out to him to come and sit down. He appealed to the man by offering Naomi's property for redemption first, without mentioning Ruth. Then he proceeded to tell the kinsman about Ruth. The nearest kinsman could not redeem her or his own inheritance would be marred. How could this be?

1. It would cause strife in the family.
2. There would be more children.
3. The financial burden would be greater.

Sometimes people will not get saved, because they are afraid of marring their worldly inheritance. What if their family cuts them off? What if their parents write them out of the will? Satan likes us to avoid pleasing the Lord and keeps us worried about temporal things instead of eternal rewards!

Why couldn't the nearest kinsman redeem? Because he was a type of the Law and the Law can never redeem. The nearest kinsman was unable to redeem. Boaz was a type of Christ and acted in Ruth's behalf as her mediator. We see many of Christ's attributes exhibited in Boaz's life. The deal was sealed by plucking off the shoe, symbolizing the yielding of the right that was his to tread upon the land.

Ruth married Boaz. She was no longer Ruth, the Moabitess. Imagine her joy when she conceived a son! She had taken the first step, and God was rewarding her for it! Ruth 4:13 says, ". . . the Lord gave her conception." Naomi was also rewarded by becoming a grandmother for the first time and was able to nurse the babe. The child was a comfort to her, and the family name was carried on.

The neighbors named the child Obed. Obed became the father of Jesse who was the father of David, in the lineage of Christ!

Conclusions

The whole book of Ruth pictures Christ as our Redeemer and His interest in Jews and Gentiles alike. The book of Ruth also portrays the requirements for a Kinsman-Redeemer:

1. He must be a near kinsman.	Christ took on humanity.
2. He must be willing to redeem.	Christ was a willing sacrifice.
3. He must be able to redeem.	Christ **is able** to save!
4. He must be free.	Christ was free from sin.
5. He must have the price of redemption.	Christ gave His life for our redemption.

Ruth did not display any special gifts. She was not "loud and showy," not a great leader or a prophetess, but "merely a domesticated girl clinging to a domestic affection." *(Matheson, p. 191)*

This story shows how God can use calamities in our life and turn them into something good. Though we experience grief, poverty, or illness, God gives grace through the suffering. David was witness to this as he stated in Psalm 57:1: ". . . in the shadow of thy wings will I make my refuge, until these calamities be overpast."

Whatever calamity we face, the story of Ruth shows us that God is still in control and follows us even during our wanderings. Though we may face days without hope, dark tunnels without an end, and streets filled with despair, God remains in control!

Through Ruth, we also learn that God is our Provider. We need only ask and be diligent to seek Him. If we trust in Him, He will reward that trust. Love returns love! God is no respecter of persons. He loves the foreigner and the outcast. His matchless grace reaches across any barrier.

And, last but not least, beware of going to the "far country and getting a whipping."

Ruth's Roles

1. Housewife
2. Widow
3. Stranger
4. Heathen
5. Convert
6. Gleaner
7. Wife
8. Mother
9. Daughter-in-law

Ruth's Character Traits

1. Meekness
2. Poise
3. Submissiveness
4. Persistence
5. Gracefulness
6. Determination
7. Unselfishness
8. Decisiveness
9. Modesty
10. Courtesy
11. Purity
12. Bravery
13. Ambition
14. Patience
15. Loyalty
16. Reliability

Notes

Chapter 4

MARY AND MARTHA
"Spirituality and Practicality"

Facts		
	Mary	**Martha**
Husband:	None known	None known, Simon?
Children:	None known	None known
Occupation:	Homemaker	Homemaker
Her name means	Bitterness	"Lady," Mistress

This New Testament story takes place in a small village called Bethany, located approximately one and a half miles from Jerusalem on Mt. Olivet. Relics from a local tomb reveal that Canaanites settled this area before the land was taken by the Israelites. Christ's ascension also took place near this town *(Luke 24:50-51)* and He often visited friends here. The village was generally known as "Lazarus' village," or the "house of misery." *(Davis Dictionary, p. 93; New Unger's, p. 162)*

Family and Friends (Luke 10:38-39; John 11:1-2)

The story opens with a peek into a family setting composed of Mary, Martha, and Lazarus. They all lived in the same home and it appears that Jesus was a friend with these people, as Martha "received him into her house." *(Luke 10:38)* Jesus had no earthly home at this time, so He probably enjoyed the fellowship of this family. Perhaps it was a place of refreshment and relaxation for Him.

We already see differences between the two sisters as Martha received Him, and Luke 10:39 tells us that Mary sat at His feet. Martha was the extrovert - busy externally, a doer who loved to be involved in everything. Mary was the introvert - busy internally, an observer who loved to listen to and meditate on Jesus' teachings.

These two sisters had a sick brother, Lazarus, but Scripture does not reveal how long he had been ill. Perhaps Jesus' coming to visit was a bright spot in their day.

Faith or Frenzy   (Psa. 27:4; Matt. 6:25, 33-34; Luke 10:38-42; John 6:27; Rom. 10:17; 1 Cor. 7:35)

Martha entertained Christ and possibly the disciples also as Luke 10:38 says, "as **they** went." This meant that Martha may have had thirteen unexpected guests to dinner! Did this fluster her? How would you react to thirteen unexpected guests for a meal? Scripture reveals her frustration as it states, "But Martha was cumbered about much serving." *(Luke 10:40)* Cumbered means "distracted." If you have ever had a large unexpected group to a meal, you can sympathize with Martha. It appears that she had no opportunity to prepare ahead of time.

Her sister, Mary, had started to help her, but became so interested in talking with Jesus that Martha was left to do all of the work! Martha became so upset that she decided to approach Jesus about the matter. Didn't anyone care that she was doing all of the work? Displaying self-pity and an aggressive spirit, she asked the Lord if He cared and told Him to tell Mary to help! Was Martha jealous? Luke 10:39 seems to indicate that she had also sat at Jesus' feet.

Jesus mildly rebuked her, telling her she was anxious and troubled about many things! He told her only one thing was needed. Ryrie, along with other authors, interprets this verse in Luke 10:42 as meaning only one simple dish was necessary for the meal. *(Ryrie, p. 1461)* Perhaps Martha wished to provide a variety of elaborate and tempting dishes instead of keeping her hospitality simple and enjoying her guests. Though her motive was sincere, she was missing the much-needed fellowship with the Lord.

Jesus said Mary had chosen that which could not be taken away from her. "The many things she was troubled about were needless while the one thing she neglected was needful." Martha was allowing her outward activities to hinder her spiritually. Isn't that just like us today? Instead of making our daily devotional time with the Lord a priority, we often allow e-mail, internet, shopping, phone calls, chores, errands, etc. to hinder that time. A church may place more emphasis on music than the Word of God or become involved in ministering to the needy (community endeavors) instead of soul-winning. We may be involved in good things while neglecting the best. Are we, like Martha, robbing ourselves of "inner communion" with Christ? Jesus did not rebuke her for her activity. He rebuked her for thinking **her** duties were more important than her sister's choice. Was He really saying to her:

> "Martha, how can you mingle the primary and secondary issues in such a manner? How can you become lost in things of minor importance while I am in your home? Martha, don't you understand that I came in the first place to serve? Not to be served? Don't you see that I am much more interested in you than in shelter and food? I do appreciate your hospitality, but My first concern is for Martha, not the hostess. Martha, you are so efficient and wise – why must you do everything, even the smallest detail, by yourself? Don't you understand that I prefer a simple meal anyway? In My Kingdom priority is given to spiritual matters. Examine yourself. Know your own heart. Look at things from My point of view."
>
> (Karssen, Book 1, p. 161-162)

Second Corinthians 10:12 admonishes us that comparing ourselves among ourselves is not wise. Martha let her busyness hinder her from fellowship with the Lord. As ladies, are we content to keep our gatherings and hospitality simple, or does our pride force us to prepare to the nth degree, sacrificing precious time with the Lord?

Mary, on the other hand, turned Christ's visit into a spiritual advantage. She sat at His feet, paid close attention, demonstrated submission, and had a willingness to learn. "If we sit with Him at His feet now, we shall sit with Him on His throne shortly." *(Matthew Henry)* She was swift to hear!

Mary and Martha both sought to please Jesus. Martha showed respect by wanting only the best for Him and His friends. She likewise demonstrated a servant's heart. She could have had servants do the work, but wanted to do it herself. Spurgeon said, ". . . they both agreed in their design; they differed in their way of carrying it out."

How about you? Is your design or motive only to please the Lord? Are you carrying it out in the proper manner? As busy homemakers and servants in the local church, you **cannot** keep giving out unless you are taking in. Soon there will be nothing to give out and you will become angry and bitter that you are doing more than everyone else. "Why can't others do all the things I am doing?" A "martyr's complex" is a terrible attitude to develop and is often manifested as a "chip on the shoulder." Where does it start? It starts when you keep giving out and not taking in. Fatigue and discouragement set in, which often loosens the tongue, causing murmuring and gossip. Self-pity rules and a miserable cycle is started. What a valuable lesson we learn from these two Bible sisters! Do not let your good designs be turned into wrong attitudes. Seek to maintain a balance between your physical, domestic, and spiritual responsibilities.

Illness and Death   (John 11:1-5, 14, 17)

Shortly after this episode, sorrow and grief struck this modest home in Bethany. Lazarus became ill and the sisters sent for Jesus, showing their close relationship with Him and demonstrating their faith that He could do something. When

Jesus heard what was happening, He said that Lazarus' sickness would not be unto death. John 11:5 verified once again Jesus' close relationship with this family, as it says, "Now Jesus loved Martha, and her sister, and Lazarus."

Though Jesus had said this sickness was not unto death, by the time He arrived in Bethany four days later, Lazarus had died and had been buried. Imagine the grief of these sisters! Their only brother and the man of the house gone! What would they do?

Martha's Reaction (John 11:19-28)

Martha once again demonstrated her impetuosity by running to Jesus. Her natural temper was now to her advantage. It kept the grief from overtaking her, and she received comfort sooner than Mary did because of her forwardness. Don't we often tell people who are grieving to stay busy?

Martha told Jesus that if He had been there, Lazarus would not have died. She did not hesitate and was not afraid to express her opinion. Notice that she kind of complained and placed the burden for her brother's death on the Lord.

Though she demonstrated faith, her faith had an **"if"** clause in it. "If thou hadst been here . . ." *(John 11:21)* Is she showing faith and trust here? She insinuated that His timing was off and that he was late—tardy! She probably did not expect a miracle, as no one had ever been raised from the dead before in her generation. We do see her manifesting a measure of faith, though, that Jesus might yet be able to do something! In John 11:22, she says that she knew "whatsoever thou wilt ask of God, God will give it thee." Jesus told her that Lazarus would rise again. He managed to get Martha to look at what "shall be," not at what "had been." Are you living in the "had beens?" Are former memories holding you captive and keeping you from seeing what "shall be?" Christ wants to set you free from that bondage. Many memories are good, but we are not to become paralyzed by them and continue to live in the past.

Martha showed her belief in the resurrection of the future, not realizing He was talking about the present. *(John 11:24)* How could this help her present affliction? She needed help for the sorrowful situation she currently faced! Aren't we prone to live for the moment?

Jesus proceeded to explain the gospel to her and asked her if she believed. She affirmed her belief. "Her statement of faith was made before she had any inkling that Jesus would raise her brother from the dead." *(Jensen)* The Word of God guided her, and the authority of Christ grounded her. She hurried away to get Mary, not even taking time for her statement of faith to set in! How ironic this was! Martha was usually trying to draw Mary **away** from Jesus. Now she sought to bring Mary **to** Jesus!

Mary's Reaction   (John 11:20-21; 28-33)

Mary's temperament had become a snare to her in this situation. As she sat still in the house, she was unable to cope with her grief as well as Martha had. Though she withdrew, she reacted promptly to Christ's call of her. Jesus was concerned about her grief, and so were her many friends. The Jews had gone to her home to comfort her, and when she left the house, they thought she was going to the grave to mourn.

Mary's reaction upon seeing Christ was one of reverence and devotion. She fell at His feet and said exactly the same words that Martha had said: "If thou hadst been here, my brother had not died." *(John 11:32)* Remember, she and Martha had been grieving for four days and had probably talked together. Can't you just hear them? "Oh, if only Jesus had been here, this never would have happened! Why didn't He get here sooner?"

Jesus did not attempt to teach Mary more, like He had done with Martha. Perhaps Mary already knew from the hours she had spent at His feet. Even in her grief, Mary brought others to

Christ. Her comforters, the unbelieving Jews, had come with her and evidenced her love for the Lord.

Jesus' Reaction   (John 11:33-38; Rom. 12:15; Gal. 6:2)

Notice that Christ had human feelings and reacted to their grief by groaning in His spirit, by being troubled, and by weeping. Grieving is normal! Some of the unbelieving Jews even recognized His love, while others denied His power to help. We see His humanity clearly demonstrated in this passage.

Christ wept with them, just as Scripture commands us to do in Romans 12:15. How do we react when someone is grief-stricken? Do we avoid them because we do not know what to say? Is the situation too awkward for us? A lady experiencing grief needs another lady to weep with her, to hug her, to call her, to listen to her. Do not be afraid of grief! It is a process we will all experience sooner or later in our lives. It is an opportunity for us to live out the Scripture and help bear another's burden. *(Gal. 6:2)* Let Christ use you to help your sister in grief.

The Miracle   (John 11:22, 39-44)

At the graveside, Jesus told them to remove the stone. Martha, again speaking her mind, objected to this. She knew that by now the body would have a foul odor. Was she abandoning her previous hope that Jesus could do something for Lazarus? Was she speaking without thinking again? Was her spirit of perfectionism showing, as she would be embarrassed by the smell? Christ gently reproved her and reminded her of His promise. He called out with a loud voice: "Lazarus, come forth." *(John 11:43)* Lazarus walked out of the tomb, much to the astonishment of the people present. Imagine Mary and Martha's joy! No one had ever seen anything like it!

What miracle is the Lord waiting to perform in your life? The only object in the way was the stone to the tomb. Is there a stone in your path hindering a miracle? Perhaps you have a stone of bitterness, resentment, or false guilt. Maybe there is a stone of a bad habit that you need to remove. Only you know what the stone is, and only you can remove it. Why don't you act by faith like the people did at Lazarus' graveside? Why don't you remove that stone and let God work a miracle in your life? Experience the same joy that Mary, Martha, and Lazarus experienced.

Servants' Hearts (Matt. 26: 6-7, 13; Mark 14:3; Luke 7:37-38, 10:38; John 12:1-3, 7)

John 12 shows us that Jesus once again visited this home in Bethany. This would be His farewell visit as it was only six days before the Passover. The family made Him a nice meal as a celebration dinner. We see Martha once again serving.

Mary served in a different way this time, though she was once again at His feet. She took very expensive ointment and anointed His feet. Ryrie tells us that this ointment cost about 300 days of wages for a rural worker, perhaps around sixty dollars. The shattering of the box represented Christ's body, broken with a beautiful fragrance remaining. Mary's offering demonstrated her generous love. She gave only the best. She used her own hands showing a submissive love.

Was this the same woman with the alabaster box? The Matthew and Mark accounts say His head was anointed. The Luke account describes the woman as a sinner and also says Christ was eating in a Pharisee's house. Some speculate that Martha was either the daughter, wife, or widow of Simon the leper *(Matt. 26:6)* as he lived in Bethany, too, and Luke 10:38 says she received Christ into **her** house. We can only speculate.

Martha made no objection to the anointing. Perhaps she had contributed to the purchase. If Matthew 26:13 refers to Mary, Christ said that the anointing would be remembered throughout future years. Again, in human eyes, Mary seemed impractical, but Christ defended her action.

Conclusions

Though Martha and Mary had their problems and entirely different personalities, both ladies served the Lord with the talents they did have. "Some provide the oil for the lamps in God's church, and others light those lamps." *(Kuyper)*

Both appear to have been affluent or wealthy women by their provisions for their guests, the number of their guests, and the costly ointment used in the anointing. If they were not affluent, then they knew what sacrificial giving was all about.

Martha ministered to Jesus' physical needs of hunger and weariness; whereas, Mary ministered more to Jesus' emotional needs. Mary was a scholar and a follower, but Martha was more aggressive and a "take charge" person. These types of people see more efficient ways of getting things done and tend to interrupt and find fault. Christ tried to help her direct this.

Both serving and learning are important. We need a balance in our Christian lives. Spurgeon said, "No man can be spiritually healthy who does not meditate and commune . . . no man on the other hand, is as he should be unless he is active and diligent in holy service." Remember, that faith without works is dead.

We also need to beware of the "Martha spirit."

1. Concerned with outward show, things, pointing to self.
2. Censuring others who want to make a stand for the "old ways."
3. Claiming so many things as necessary to our church work.
4. Contentment with activity.

Remember in all three situations, Mary was at Christ's feet! We need to cultivate a "Mary spirit."

1. Personal communion with Christ, preventing mechanical service to Him.
2. Purifying our motives and strengthening our purpose.
3. Powerful service due to our closer walk with the Lord.
4. Planned and thoughtful service.

"It will be an evil day for us when we trust in the willing and the running, and practically attempt to do without the Holy Spirit."

Spurgeon

Mary's Roles

1. Scholar
2. Servant
3. Mediator
4. Homemaker

Mary's Character Traits

1. Meekness
2. Humility
3. Unselfishness

Martha's Roles

1. Servant
2. Supervisor
3. Organizer
4. Homemaker
5. Perfectionist

Martha's Character Traits

1. Impulsiveness
2. Hospitality
3. Faithfulness
4. Courage
5. Aggressiveness

Chapter 5

MARY MAGDALENE

Facts	
Husband:	None known
Children:	None known
Occupation:	None known
Her name means	Mary – "Bitterness"
	Magdala – "Watchtower; a plaiter of hair"

Scant details are given concerning the personal life of Mary Magdalene. We do find from Scripture, however, that she came from the town of Magdala, also known as Magadan. This town was located three miles from Capernaum on the west coast of the Sea of Galilee. It was a rich town known for its dye-works and textiles. Though rich in material goods, the town had serious spiritual needs and was known for it immorality and harlotry. We meet Mary Magdalene in this setting, a lady with a serious physical and mental need.

Healing By Jesus   (Mark 16:9; Luke 8:1-2)

Mary Magdalene was afflicted with seven devils. Luke 8:2 also calls them "evils spirits and infirmities." We can only imagine the torment this woman faced day and night! Perhaps she could not rest or take care of her physical appearance. She probably could not work or take care of her home either. People may have shunned and avoided her, not understanding her condition.

Though seven is the number of perfection, it was not the perfection you and I know. Was she a "perfect slave to bad passions?" Nowhere in Scripture is she called a prostitute, though some link her with the sinning woman in Luke 7 who washed Jesus' feet. The Catholic Church fostered this idea in 1324 by calling its home for fallen women, "Magdalen House." The Scripture never tells us that Mary Magdalene was a harlot. The reputation of her town seems to have been thrust upon her. Throughout the Bible, we find immoral ladies identified, such as Rahab, the harlot, the woman at the well with five husbands, and the woman taken in adultery. Wouldn't Scripture have identified this with Mary Magdalene if God wanted us to know it?

From other Biblical accounts, we know demon possession was a terrible experience to endure. People who were affected cast themselves on the ground, cursed, and called out against men of God. They were not in control of their thoughts or actions and suffered immensely. It was to this lady that our caring and compassionate Christ demonstrated His great mercy! We are not given the details of her healing, only that the Lord cast out seven devils. Imagine the relief and freedom from bondage this woman experienced! God's healing power freed her from Satan's horrible stronghold on her life. She was free to serve Christ!

Perhaps you face some stronghold in your life. Are you letting your past affect your present service for the Lord? Does Satan keep invading your mind with self-condemning thoughts and feelings of hopelessness? Do you always feel unworthy and not "good enough?" Satan loves to keep us immobilized, paralyzing us with fear and rendering us useless in our service for the Lord. As believers in Christ, we need to claim Romans 8:1, which says, "There is therefore now **no condemnation** to them which are in Christ Jesus, who walk not after the flesh, but after the Spirit." What a wonderful hope we have as believers! Dear lady, have you accepted Jesus Christ as your Lord and Saviour? If so, then refuse to allow Satan to keep deluding you and using your mind as his playground. Claim Romans 8:1 and free yourself to serve!

Let's see what Mary Magdalene did with her liberty.

Ministering by the Wayside (Mark 15:40-41; Luke 8:2-3)

Mary took her newfound freedom and totally committed herself to following Jesus. Why? Did she remember the days and nights of mental torment, the weeks and months of hallucinations and delusional fears? She knew she could not minimize Satan's power. Her closeness to God would be her defense. What protection and provision He offers! She also followed Him out of love and gratitude. Because she had been helped, she wanted to help: " . . . freely ye have received, freely give." *(Matt. 10:8b)* She also knew that Christ had given her much: " . . . For unto whomsoever much is given, of him shall be much required. . ." *(Luke 12:48b)*

Serving Jesus became her **first** priority. She ministered to Him with what substance she had. Because of her great commitment, some scholars believe she may have been single, freeing her to leave her home and follow Jesus. Whatever the case, we find her mentioned nineteen times in the gospels. Fourteen of those times we find her ministering with women. The other five times she is found alone and present at the death and Resurrection of Christ.

What new purpose she had found! All of her energies were now directed to ministering and caring for others!

Standing by the Cross (Matt. 27:55-56; Mark 15:40; Luke 23:49; John 19:25)

Mary Magdalene faithfully followed her Lord to the Cross. We see her with a group of godly women including Jesus' own mother. Perhaps she had made friends with these women and was now there to show her love and support. Notice that we do not see her "hanging out" with the old group from Magdala. She had chosen a new path and new friends. How are your friendships doing? Are you running with the "old crowd?" We as ladies need other godly lady friends! Godly friends will encourage us because we have companionship as we walk in the right direction together. We can share the blessings of the Lord with our friends. Our Lord knew friends were important as He said in Proverbs 18:24: "A man that hath friends must show himself friendly: and there is a friend that sticketh closer than a brother." He likewise instructed us to make no friendship with an angry person. *(Prov. 22:24)*

Be careful to make friends with those who want to please the Lord and obey Scripture. Remember that Amnon would have done right, but he listened to a friend. *(2 Sam. 13:1-3)* If you are serious about serving the Lord, it is wise to evaluate your friendships. Do your friends lift up Christ and His name? Do they talk about godly things? Do you feel built-up and encouraged after being with them, or guilty and melancholy?

The greatest Friend we will ever have is the Lord Jesus Christ. Who else would lay down His life for us? "Greater love hath no man than this, that a man lay down his life for his friends. Ye are **my friends**, if ye do whatsoever I command you." *(John 15:13-14)* How are you doing in the friend department? Is Jesus Christ your **best Friend?** He wants to be! Can you go to Him and tell Him everything? Do you show your love for Him by keeping His commandments? Can we follow the example of Mary Magdalene and stick close to our Friend?

By following her Master to the Cross, Mary Magdalene demonstrated "sufficient feminine resilience to be able to witness the death of the Mediator." *(Kuyper)* She showed her love and loyalty to her Master. Did she perhaps wonder why Jesus did not help Himself? She had witnessed His divine power so many times! How difficult it must have been for her to see her Friend die! However, the Lord was her strength. "Even those of the weaker sex are often, by the grace of God, made strong in faith, that Christ's strength may be made perfect in weakness." *(Matthew Henry)*

Arriving at the Tomb

(Matt. 28:1-8; Mark 16:1-8; Luke 24:1-
10; John 20:1, 11)

Mary was about to perform her last service for the Lord. On the first day of the week, just as dawn was breaking, she, along with Mary (James' mother), Joanna, and Salome, approached the graveside. These ladies had prepared special spices to anoint their Friend's body. They were loyal friends to the end!

Upon approaching the tomb, the ladies noticed the stone was rolled away from the door of the sepulchre. They entered the tomb and saw a young man clothed in a white garment sitting on the right.

What did the angel tell the ladies? Notice that the angel gave them commands. He told them to **"fear not**, for he is risen." The ladies were then invited to **"come see** the place where the Lord lay."** They were then instructed to **"go quickly and tell** his disciples."** *(Matt. 28:5-7)* After this interlude with the angel, the final promise to the ladies was **"ye shall see Him!"** *(Matt. 28:7)* Without a doubt, these ladies experienced feelings of joy and fear according to Matthew 28:8. What an emotional event it was! Had their Friend and Lord risen from the dead? It was an unbelievable happening! Mary was probably grateful she had taken the time to go the garden early that morning.

Meeting with Jesus

(Isa. 43:1; Mark 16:9; John 10:3-4, 14, 27;
John 20:11-18)

After the other women left, Mary stood outside the tomb weeping. She just could not leave yet! Weeping, she stooped down and looked again into the tomb. How surprised she was to see two angels, "one at the head, and the other at the feet, where the body of Jesus had lain." *(John 20:12)* This time she showed no fear of the angels and actually conversed with them after they asked her why she was crying. She said, "Because they have taken away **my Lord** . . ." Notice once again the personal relationship she had with Him. Apparently she thought they had taken Jesus to another site. The resurrection had not "sunk in" yet!

Then, the unimaginable thing happened! Jesus Himself appeared to her and asked her why she was crying. Notice His tenderness with her, His concern, His compassion. Mary, perhaps not even turning around, asked Him if He was the gardener, and where he had taken Jesus. She was persistent in her seeking of her Master. What a lesson this is to us! Are we persistent in seeking our time with the Lord? What happens when we sit down with our Bibles? Something usually immediately occurs to distract or divert us. The phone rings, the UPS man comes, the children wake up, or we feel compelled to check our e-mail or "to do list" first. Mary was not to be distracted. She did not even turn to look at the gardener. She kept her eyes peeled on the tomb.

It was only after Jesus called her by name that she finally recognized Who had been speaking to her all along. She had been looking for the living among the dead. She had been looking in the wrong place for Him! He had been near her all the time, and she did not even know it.

Aren't we like that today? We will buy devotional books, novels, videos, tapes, and neglect opening our Bibles to discover what the Lord wants to say to us. These things are not wrong and may be of a help, but not if we leave out the best – the inspired, infallible Word of God. God is near all the time, waiting for us to cry out to Him and to have sweet fellowship with Him. He wants us to turn our eyes upon Him, to commune with Him. The Scripture says, "Be still and know that I am God . . ." *(Psa. 46:10a)*

Imagine Mary's surprise when she finally recognized her best Friend was speaking to her. Notice that He called her by her name. She was important to Him! What an honor to be the **very first person** to see the living, resurrected Jesus! She responded by calling him "Rabboni," meaning Master and showing she was under His authority. She demonstrated a submissive spirit.

This godly woman is not demeaned in Biblical Christianity. Jesus honored her submissive spirit by choosing her to carry the good news to His brethren. What would today's "women libbers" think of that? Not only was she the first **eyewitness** of the Resurrection, but also the **first witness**! Amazing! "Mary Magdalene, who followed Christ to the last in His humiliation, met Him with the first in His exaltation." *(Matthew Henry)*

Carrying the Good News (Matt. 28:10-11; Mark 16:10-11; Luke 24:9-11; John 20:18)

Mary Magdalene immediately obeyed her Lord and ran to tell the good news! She now had a new purpose and a new goal. Notice that Jesus had told her not to be afraid to do it. What a lesson to us in witnessing! Do we obey the Lord and tell others? We have the greatest story the world has ever heard. Are we afraid to share it? Can we give a tract at the store or a word of witness?

Remember here that Mary Magdalene was sent to tell the Lord's disciples as well as others. Would they believe her? She could not worry about that. She was the voice box for the Lord. No, the disciples did not believe her. They thought it was all just idle talk. Perhaps they knew her past history and thought her mind was acting up again. However, Mary did not let that deter her from the assignment. She knew the truth and was not afraid to share it! She overcame human fear and completed her assignment. We as ladies must do the same today in witnessing to others for His glory!

Conclusions

What a beautiful example Mary Magdalene is to us! She is mentioned in all four gospels and was the first person to see the resurrected Saviour. Constantly active and ambitious, she demonstrated her dedication and commitment in three ways:

1. **Trust**   She followed Christ when others fled.
2. **Service**   She was a need-meeter.
3. **Witness**   She was bold in sharing.

She ministered in three ways also.

1. **Financially**   She gave of her substance.
2. **Sympathetically**   She stood vigil.
3. **Memorially**   She prepared to anoint His body.

The Greek church says she died at Ephesus, but Westerners say she was carried up to Heaven in the arms of angels. There is no Scripture to verify these speculations.

"No woman played a more majestic role in Christ's last days." *(Edith Deen)* "She owed much, gave much, loved much, served much." *(Lockyer)* God looks with favor upon women who totally dedicate themselves to Him. Mary Magdalene had that favor. Do you want favor with God? Then give much, love much, and serve much!

Mary Magdalene

Her Roles

1. Servant
2. Witness
3. Friend
4. Traveler

Her Character Traits

1. Persistence
2. Obedience
3. Ambition
4. Submission
5. Loyalty

Chapter 6

DORCAS
(Tabitha)
The Lady with a Needle in Her Hand

Facts	
Husband:	None known
Children:	None known
Occupation:	Homemaker, Seamstress
Her name means	"Gazelle"

Dorcas lived in the picturesque city of Joppa, a small seaport located thirty miles from Jerusalem on the Mediterranean coast. Joppa was famous for its orchards, its tanneries, and its soap-making industry. The town was partially filled with foreigners who spoke mainly the Greek language; hence, this lady was known as Dorcas to these residents, and as Tabitha (her Jewish name) to the church. The town, Joppa, became known as Jaffa and is called Tel Aviv, today.

Her Heart   (Acts 9:36, 39, 41; Jam. 1:26-27; 2:15-17)

The first word the Bible uses about Dorcas is the word "disciple." She belonged to the early New Testament church, and kindness seemed to be her life motto. We see Dorcas putting action to her faith. She was a need-seeker and a need-meeter, freely giving of her time **and** resources. The Scripture uses the words "full of good works and almsdeeds."

She was a capable seamstress, and her gifts of clothing to others consumed hours of her time. Remember that there were no sewing machines in those days, so Dorcas lovingly hand-stitched the garments that she so willingly gave away.

Perhaps she was a widow or a single lady as no family or children are ever mentioned. However, instead of living in self-pity or despair, she found the secret of joy and happiness—that of serving the Lord and giving to others. Manifesting a living portrayal of Galatians 6:10 and 1 Timothy 5:3, she ministered in a practical way to those of the "household of faith" and also honored the widows.

There were many widows in Joppa due to the coastal area and storms. Many men's lives were lost due to their work on the sea, thus providing an opportunity to Dorcas. If she was a widow, she could totally empathize with these dear ladies and take them under her wing.

Dorcas was a lady of action. She did not sit around and talk about her plan or expect others to carry out the plan. Like the Proverbs 31 lady, she was always working and serving. Her time was not wasted on coffee breaks, shopping, or her own hobbies. No, indeed, her talent and material wealth were dedicated to those less fortunate than her, and they loved her for it!

However, we need to beware of having Dorcas' deeds and not her faith. Her faith was the mainspring of her works, not her works the road to her faith! Notice Scripture mentions **first** that she was a disciple. Her works were secondary, though she was **full of them!**

> "Giving of alms, and the making of garments in themselves gain no merit with God, who, first of all, claims our hearts **before** our talents ... and so the hands that dispensed alms and made garments were inwardly inspired by Him whose hands were nailed to a tree." *(Lockyer, p. 46-47)*

So it was with Dorcas! She loved God and served Him whole-heartedly. She showed her faith by her works—by her hands!

Her Hurting

(Acts 9:37-39)

Much to the dismay of those who loved her, Dorcas contracted an illness and died. Notice what a loving reputation she had with other women. They came to wash her and anoint her, to prepare her body for burial. The Bible says they laid her in an upper chamber. How they lovingly performed these tender mercies to her. Look at what she had done for them! They were still wearing the clothing she had made them!

Evidently, the disciples knew this lady or had heard the news of her death. Perhaps they themselves had benefited personally from her kindness. Whatever the case, they hurriedly sent two men to Lydda, a town ten miles away, to fetch Peter. A pastor— a man of God—was needed at this time of crisis—this time of grief and heartbreak.

Her Healing

(Acts 9:39-42)

Did Peter hear the weeping as he approached the house? As he entered the upstairs chamber, the ladies proceeded to show him all of the "coats and garments, which Dorcas made." What a loss they were now facing! Sending them out of the room, Peter knelt down and prayed. He called her by her Jewish name, "Tabitha," saying, "Arise." Dorcas opened her eyes and sat up. Imagine the celebration of joy that occurred when Peter presented her to these saints and widows! Obviously, Christ's resurrection was still fresh in their minds! What thanksgiving and praise ascended to the Lord as He once again manifested His supernatural, healing power! He had given Dorcas back to them!

Great results from this miracle were widespread! Dorcas' suffering and death produced salvations as "many believed in the Lord." Who knows what joy will come from our suffering? It is important to be faithful during our tests and trials, as others are watching, and we are the living epistles they read. Many had read Dorcas' life epistle, and now the news spread far and wide, affecting many for Christ. Could our faithfulness during times of sorrow and grief also point others to Him?

Notice in verse 43 that Peter tarried many days. Perhaps there were many new converts to disciple, and there were probably many added to the church there in Joppa.

Conclusions

Though we have only a brief account of Dorcas' life, it is a powerful message. She is the only adult lady mentioned in Scripture who was raised from the dead. Scripture says nothing negative about her, and her testimony lives on today. Many sewing societies are named for her. Not only was she **full** of good works, but she also **maintained** good works. "And let ours also learn to **maintain** good works for necessary uses, that they be not **unfruitful.**" (Titus 3:14) Maintain means "to preserve; to keep in existence or **continuance**; to keep or hold against attack." Because Dorcas stayed busy with good works, she preserved herself from Satan's attack. When we can or preserve food, we are keeping it from the contamination of bacteria and harmful elements. Do you want to be preserved from Satanic attack? Then maintain good works!

Though her ministry was "behind the scenes," it produced great fruit for the Lord. Do not ever think your "behind-the-scenes" ministry is unimportant. We are all needed in the body of Christ, and He is no respecter of persons. You may say, "Well, I cannot sing or teach like so-and-so. All I can do is clean the church or work in the nursery." These are very important ministries and affect others for the Lord. Do sinners want to come into a dirty church? Will a crying baby keep someone from accepting Christ? Keep cleaning the church and working in the nursery for the Lord! Do not let Satan delude you into thinking your ministry does not count! Dorcas could only sew, yet God thought it important enough to include her biography in the New Testament.

Dorcas used what was in her hand, her sewing needle. Moses used his rod. David used his sling. The little boy used his lunch. Mary used her box of ointment. Martha used her pots and pans. What has the Lord placed within your hand? Is it sewing, music, cooking, gardening, crafts, etc? Are you using that talent for Him, or have you buried it only for yourself? Do you compare your one talent with someone else's many talents? Dorcas did not do this. She took her sewing skill and used it for God. So, get busy! Develop that talent and use it for God as Dorcas did! "She who does good for good's sake (and God's sake!) seeking neither praise nor reward, is sure of both in the end." *(George)*

Her reputation of providing garments opened a door for sharing the garment of salvation with many! Dorcas was **faithful** and **fruitful!** What will you be remembered for? For your faith and good works? For your merciful, unselfish giving to others?

> "Now therefore **perform the doing of it**; that as there was a readiness to will, so there may be a performance also out of that which ye have." *(2 Cor. 8:11)*

Use What God Has Put Within Your Hand!

Dorcas' Roles

1. Servant
2. Seamstress
3. Philanthropist
4. Disciple

Dorcas' Character Traits

1. Unselfishness
2. Kindness
3. Mercy
4. Faithfulness
5. Fruitfulness

Faithful & Fruitful
Women of the Bible, volume 2

Notes

Chapter 7

RHODA

Facts	
Husband:	None known
Children:	None known
Occupation:	Servant
Her name means	"Rose"

Persistent Persecution   (Acts 12:1-11)

The short yet important biography of Rhoda begins during a time of severe persecution within the early church. This persecution had moved from the hands of religious leaders to those of government leaders. Politics was now involved as King Herod determined to use brutal means to "vex" the church. Acts 12:1 says that he "stretched forth his hands to vex certain of the church." The words "stretched" and "hands" show us that this was a very active work, and Herod meant business. Demonstrating his jealousy, he hand-picked the leaders he wanted to remove from the scene.

One of these leaders was James, the brother of John. Herod determined to bring the Christians under his thumb. After killing James and watching the favorable effect on the Jews, Herod imprisoned Peter. Possessing a paranoid nature and knowing of other miraculous events surrounding the disciples, Herod placed Peter under four quarternions of soldiers. Upon hearing of his capture, the early believers were vigilant in their prayers for Peter. This was their leader! He was in desperate trouble!

Though Peter was a step from death, he had no problem with insomnia. Acts 12:6 tells us that he slept between two soldiers.

What looked impossible to man was possible with God! God intervened and delivered Peter. An angel of the Lord awoke him and instructed Peter to follow him. Immediately Peter's chains fell off. He dressed himself and followed the angel right out of the prison house. Though he thought he was having a vision, Peter did not fail to obey.

His deliverance is a picture of our redemption by Christ. How He longs to deliver us from the chains of darkness and the clutches of sin! It grieves His heart to see us bound and hindered by sin! He approaches us just as He did Peter. First, the Holy Spirit convicts and sheds light on our sin. Then He renews our will. We have to take that step toward Him. Finally, like Peter, He commands us to "gird" ourselves and to follow Him. Will we obey and give Him first place in our life?

Dear lady, you may never have truly been born again. Do you have a 100 percent assurance that you are ready to meet the Lord? All you need to do is: accept the fact that you are a sinner *(Rom. 3:23);* realize that there is a price God exacts on that sin *(Rom. 6:23);* believe that God sent His Son, Jesus Christ, to die on the Cross and pay that price for you *(Rom. 5:8);* and ask Christ to forgive you of your sins and take you to Heaven when you die. *(Rom. 10:13)*

Or you may already be a Christian, but there may be some sin hindering your walk with the Lord. Confess that sin today and have renewed fellowship with Him. *(1 John 1:8-9)* Do not let Satan imprison you and keep you in a state of guilt and turmoil. Peter's chains fell off, and the angel led him out of that prison.

Prevailing Prayer (Acts 12:5, 12-17)

Mary, the sister of Barnabas and the mother of John Mark, was hosting a late night prayer meeting in her home. Persecution had driven these early believers to their knees, and Scripture states that "many were gathered together praying." *(Acts 12:12)* These believers were fervent in prayer and wanted their leader released. "The effectual fervent prayer of a righteous man availeth much." *(Jam. 5:16)* They prayed unceasingly for Peter.

Enter Rhoda... We see Rhoda participating in this prayer meeting. She is called a damsel, meaning a "female slave" or "servant," a "bondmaid." It is thought that she may have come from Cyprus since Mary's brother was from Cyprus, and Rhoda may have moved to Jerusalem when the family did. Whatever the case, she was not only a servant, but it appears she, like the rest of the family, was a believer.

After Peter came to his senses and meditated on the miracle that had just occurred in his life, he set off for Mary's house. Perhaps he knew of the prayer meeting, or maybe he was used to holding services for the believers there himself. Knowing he would be welcome, we see him on Mary's porch knocking at her door.

Rhoda, ever faithful at her post, heard the knocking and went to answer the door. After hearing Peter's voice, she became so excited that she did not even open the door, but ran back to tell the others that Peter was there! Amazing! Their prayers had been answered! We see joy and spontaneity displayed in her character. She rejoiced and ran with the good news. Perhaps she had prayed, believing and expecting an answer to her prayers. Notice that she recognized Peter's voice!

The others told her she was mad or a "maniac." She did not let their thoughts sway her and insisted that it was so. "But she constantly affirmed that it was even so." *(Acts 12:15)* They were not going to steal her joy! The unbelieving prayer warriors told her it was Peter's angel. The Jews held the belief that each person had a guardian angel. Who did they think was at the door? Did they think it was:

1. Someone running an errand for Peter?
2. Peter's guardian angel called a "good genius," one
    who actually impersonated the individual?
    (a superstitious belief commonly held in those days)

3. An angel known as a "ward" appearing as a premonition of Peter's death?
4. The enemy posing as Peter?

They finally went to the door and opened it! Imagine their astonishment when they saw Peter standing there! Rhoda's persistence had paid off! Their prayers had been answered right in front of their very eyes! "And it shall come to pass, that before they call, I will answer; and while they are yet speaking, I will hear." *(Isa. 65:24)* Isn't that just like us today? We pray, and when God answers, we are amazed. Spurgeon said, "If the Lord wants to surprise His people, He has only at once to give them an answer. No sooner do they receive an answer than they say, 'Who would have thought it?' " *(Lockyer, p. 142)* What a perfect description this is of the early believers and Peter's miracle!

Peter told them the story of the miracle and told them to go share the good news with their other brethren. In a fit of rage, Herod had the prison keepers put to death. Little did he know that his demise was soon to occur. Days later, as he sat dressed in his royal apparel and was puffed up with his own pride, the angel of the Lord struck him, "and he was eaten of worms and gave up the ghost." *(Acts 12:23)*

Prolific Propagation   (Acts 12:18-25)

Because of the early believers' persecution and prayers, the gospel spread. "The courage and comfort of the martyrs and God's owning them, did more to invite people to Christianity, than their suffering did to deter them from it." *(Matthew Henry)* The seed was planted, watered, and brought forth fruit from the faithful and fervent lives of the early church.

Can the same be said of us today? We know very little about suffering for Christ like the early church and martyrs. Are we fervent in prayer for our president, pastor, and other leaders, or is our faith anemic? Do we react like the early believers did when God answered their prayers, or do we even practice fervent praying? Does our faithfulness produce fruit like Rhoda's did?

Conclusions

Though God had opened the doors of the prison for Peter, Rhoda, in her excitement, failed to open the door to Mary's home the first time. God has opened the door of our prison. Are we letting Him break our chains of sin and bring us out of our prison?

Rhoda was doing a routine task at her post of duty when she witnessed a great miracle. She is known for one main thing – opening the door for Peter. She recognized his voice. Do you recognize God's voice? She ran to share the good news with others. Do you run with the good news? Her exuberance and joy led others to the door to see for themselves. Are you leading others to the door to witness the miracle of salvation in their lives? Rhoda was known for one event. What one event will you be known for?

Rhoda's persistence paid off. Often we give up in witnessing to others due to our own impatience. When we see few or little results, we become discouraged and fail to continue. It was not so with Rhoda. She stood her ground until the group went to the door.

Are you faithful to your post of duty and to fervent prayer? Oh, that we might be praying and godly women, intercessors for our family and church.

Rhoda's Roles

1. Servant
2. Witness
3. Prayer warrior

Rhoda's Character Traits

1. Ambition
2. Determination
3. Persistence
4. Joyfulness
5. Faithfulness

Chapter 8

LYDIA

Facts	
Husband:	None known
Children:	None known
Occupation:	Businesswoman, Seller of purple
Her name means	"Bending"

Acts 16:12-15 provides the setting of our next faithful and fruitful lady. It is during Paul's second missionary journey that we meet this wealthy and successful woman.

The Lord had called Paul to go over to Macedonia. So, obeying this call, Paul traveled and arrived in Philippi, the chief city of Macedonia, "a Roman colony founded by Augustus." *(New Ungers, p. 1002)* This city was on the main highway from Rome to Asia and was known for its fertile soil and gold mines. Philippi also boasted a school of medicine and because of this, it is thought that Luke, the physician, may have been a Philippian.

After being in the city for several days without a convert, Paul may have become discouraged and doubtful. Little did he know his first convert would be a woman and how God would use this woman to help him plant the first church in Europe.

Faithful in Prayer   (Acts 16:13)

On that beautiful Sabbath morning, Lydia, along with several other women, had set aside the day for prayer and meditation. It had become a habit for these ladies to gather at the riverside every Sabbath to have a prayer service, away from the frantic pace of city life. Perhaps there was no synagogue in Philippi they could resort to, as it took ten Jewish men to organize one. *(Ryrie, p. 1569)* So, these spiritually hungry women took it upon themselves to pray and meditate.

It was to this group that Paul, Silas, Timothy, and Dr. Luke came. It did not appear to be a pre-arranged meeting, but a divine appointment by God. God knows who has a hungry heart and is ready to respond to His Word. He knew these ladies were faithful to prayer and sent Paul their way to minister to them.

Faithful in Worship (Acts 16:14)

We are now personally introduced to Lydia and discover many things about her just from this one verse of Scripture. Her name means "bending." What a perfect picture of her bending her will to that of the Lord Jesus Christ. Little did she know how her life was about to change!

Lydia was from the city of Thyatira, renowned for its purple dye. Citizens of Thyatira worshipped Apollo as a sun god. However, Lydia maintained her Jewish faith and worshipped God. Providence had brought her to Philippi to hear Paul.

It appears that she was a successful businesswoman, as Scripture tells us she was "a seller of purple." She may have had her own clothing store and possibly sold purple fabric imported from Thyatira. She was a woman of ambition and purpose. Apparently she had relocated her business. No husband is mentioned, so she may have been a widow (or single) and had to work. However, she did not let her busy work schedule prevent her from prayer and worship. Did she face persecution in the work force for her Jewish faith? If so, she did not let it discourage or deter her, and she remained reliable and dependable in her work and in her faith. God prospered her for it. Her success in business did not prevent her from the appointed time of worship.

Although Lydia was religious, she had never heard the gospel until the day Paul spoke to her. She was in the right place at the right time. Scripture tells us that the Lord opened her **heart**, and she believed "the things which were spoken of Paul."

"Conversion-work is **heart** work; it is a renewing of the heart, the inward man, the spirit of the mind . . ." *(Matthew Henry, p. 207)*

She "attended" to Paul's message. She paid attention to, applied herself, and took heed to his words. *(Zodhiates, p. 61)* Ladies, do we listen, take heed, and apply Biblical principles we hear taught? Or do we remain stubborn and set in our ways, unwilling to conform our lives to God's Word? Lydia would never regret opening her heart to the gospel.

The Word did not return void, and Lydia became Paul's first European convert! Her experience would greatly affect her family, her friends, and other citizens of Philippi.

Faithful in Works (Acts 16:15, 40)

Being a lady of action, Lydia did not hesitate, but immediately took the next step in her Christian walk. She was baptized along with her household. Had she run home and shared the good news with her family and servants? Their lives were likewise transformed, and they all obeyed the Lord in believer's baptism.

Immediately she opened her home to the missionaries. She "constrained" them to make use of her home, compelling them, forcing them, entreating them. *(Zodhiates, p. 54)* What an excitement prevailed! Her home may have held the cottage prayer meetings and the first services of the early church in Philippi.

What a haven her home became to Paul and Silas! After they were beaten, imprisoned, and released, they sought out her gracious hospitality again. Her home served as a place of peace, refreshment, and wonderful Christian fellowship. She lived out Paul's command to the believer in Romans 12:13: "Distributing to the necessity of saints; given to hospitality."

How long has it been since you have opened your home to another believer? Have you distributed to another saint's necessity? When you have pastors, evangelists, or missionaries into your home, your children get "hands on" with those people. They are able to see their humanity. They are able to ask them questions. Who knows how your children may be influenced by other men and women of God?

You may say, "Well, Lydia was a lady of means, and my home is too humble!" Jesus did not even have a home of His own, yet He demonstrated hospitality. He used whatever was available and at hand. Often His hospitality was outdoors or in another's home. He did not let a lack of material things deter Him from reaching out to others. Abraham and Sarah served their guests in a drafty tent!

We need to keep our hospitality simple and refreshing. We do not have to have a seven-course meal for our guests. They want to fellowship with us and get to know us. Sometimes a bowl of popcorn, a dessert, or a fruit and veggie tray is all that is needed! Remember to distribute to the necessity of saints!

Faithful in Fruit-Bearing   (Phil. 1:1-10)

Although we hear Lydia's name mentioned no more after this, we do see Paul commending the group of believers there in Philippians 1:1-10. Lydia is part of that group. Paul told the Philippian believers that he prayed for them and remembered their "fellowship in the gospel from the **first day** until now." *(Phil. 1:4-5)* That first day began with Lydia's conversion. Paul said he was confident that God would finish the great work He had begun in those Philippian believers and prayed for them to be filled "with the **fruits** of righteousness." Lydia faithfully portrayed Romans 12:11 where Paul exhorted the believers to be "not slothful in business; fervent in spirit; serving the Lord."

We know she bore immediate fruit after her conversion, and

it is likely that she continued to bear fruit through her faithful witness.

Conclusions

Lydia's biography leaves us with many lessons to apply to our own lives as faithful and fruitful women for the Lord.

First, though she was religious, she had no personal relationship with the Lord. Although she possessed great intelligence and many material goods, she recognized her need of a Saviour. Wealth, education, and friends did not fill the void in her heart. How is it with you? Are you religious? Perhaps you attend church and pray like Lydia did, but have never confessed your sins and trusted Christ for forgiveness. Like Lydia, being a worshipper of God is not enough. Have you taken that first step? God shows His great love and care for women and that He is no respecter of persons in the story of Lydia.

After opening her heart to the gospel, she shared her joy of the good news with her household. Are you spreading the good news? Are you faithful to distribute tracts, make phone calls, and participate in your church's soul-winning program? Is it a priority in your life? It was in Lydia's!

Lydia then took the next step after her salvation. She followed the Lord in believer's baptism. Though baptism does not save us, it is a picture to others of the decision we have made and an important step of obedience. Lydia did not question or lag behind in this step, but encouraged others to take that step with her. How about you? Have you followed the Lord in believer's baptism?

Lydia remained faithful to God regardless of her job and other business responsibilities. What about you, dear lady? Perhaps you, too, work out of the home. Do you let this affect your faithfulness to the Lord's house? Do your co-workers even know you are a Christian? Do they see a difference in you? Are you reliable and dependable? God can and will provide strength for you if you will put Him first. Make Him, not your job, your first priority. A job should never come between you and the Lord. Perhaps Lydia's successful career was due to her faithfulness in prayer and worship. Are your affections set only on things here below, or do you have eternal goals in mind?

"Lydia not only sold her dyes – she served her Saviour. Lydia was, first of all, a consecrated Christian, then a conscientious businesswoman . . ." *(Lockyer, p. 85)* She served Christ where she was, becoming a great light in Philippi, pointing her family, friends, and business associates to Christ. "Lydia's enthusiasm for God bore fruit in others' lives." *(Karssen, vol. 1, p. 190)* Her love of hospitality and sharing of her home refreshed many. Can we prioritize our lives in the same manner and emulate Lydia?

"She will ever stand among the immortal women of the Bible, for she picked up that first torch from Paul at Philippi and carried it steadfastly." *(Deen, p. 226)* May we likewise be faithful, God-fearing women who carry the torch and bear fruit for our Lord and Saviour, Jesus Christ.

Lydia's Roles

1. Businesswoman
2. Witness
3. Prayer warrior
4. Servant

Lydia's Character Traits

1. Ambition
2. Determination
3. Persistence
4. Hospitality
5. Faithfulness
6. Obedience

Chapter 9

PRISCILLA

Facts	
Husband:	Aquila
Children:	None known
Occupation:	Tentmaker; Housewife
Her name means	"Primitive, worthy, venerable;"
	"ancient, old-fashioned simplicity"

We first meet Priscilla in Corinth near the end of Paul's second missionary journey. She and her husband, Aquila, knew what it was to be persecuted. During a great anti-Semitic outbreak, Claudius had banned all Jews from Rome, forcing this couple to seek refuge in Corinth. Corinth was "the Hollywood and the Las Vegas of the Roman Empire." *(McGee, p. 592)* It was a great commercial city, the "mecca of trade between the East and the West." *(New Ungers, p. 255)* Though Corinth was a bustling and well-developed city, it was also a beehive of sin, including immorality and carnality.

Was Priscilla happy about the move to Corinth? She probably had to leave her friends, her home, and her business contacts behind. What would this new city offer her? She and Aquila's missionary training would begin here.

Her Family and Occupation   (Acts 18:1-2)

Priscilla's Roman name indicates a prominent family background, though Scripture remains silent concerning her parents. She is never mentioned apart from her husband, Aquila,

65

showing us they were a team who whole-heartedly served the Lord together.

We assume they were childless, as no children are ever mentioned. However, they did not let this fact mar or hinder their walk with the Lord. They eagerly and joyously opened their home to others, and we never see them murmuring or complaining about their lot in life.

Their secular occupation was tentmaking, so the Apostle Paul would feel quite at home with them. Though their trade was a common one, it was an honest one, and they probably developed a good reputation for their work. Perhaps that is why they relocated in Corinth, the thriving city, as they knew they would always have work there.

Her Faith and Works (Acts 18:3, 11-13, 18-19, 23-28)

Acts 18:3 tells us that Paul found this couple. We do not know how they connected. Perhaps it was through the common occupation they shared. Whatever the reason, a great friendship developed, and Paul stayed there with them for eighteen months. Paul may have led them both to the Lord and then discipled them for that period of time. Can you imagine the interesting and stimulating conversations about the Lord which may have occurred? It was a time of growth for the "Aquila family."

Priscilla was an exhorter and an encourager. She displayed great leadership potential, but always under the authority of her husband. Possessing a keen mind, she was always eager to know more about the Scripture and her walk as a believer.

When Paul was taken before Achaia, the deputy of Corinth, this did not hinder his friendship with Aquila and Priscilla. Acts 18:18 tells us that when Paul later sailed to Syria, the "Aquila family" was with him. Priscilla did not allow fear to dominate her. She followed her husband everywhere and did not base decisions on her emotions.

The entourage set off for Ephesus. Ephesus was a city with great political, economical, and religious prominence. It boasted a strategic location on major trade routes and hosted the worship of Diana. Did Priscilla want to go to Ephesus? Was she eager to move again?

After arriving in Ephesus, Paul left them there. Did he know that they would be disciplers and encouragers to the saints there? Remember, he had lived with this family for eighteen months and knew they were stable and dedicated Christians. Priscilla and Aquila rose to the occasion.

During their time in Ephesus a Jew named Apollos arrived on the scene. Though this man was "mighty in the Scriptures" and an eloquent speaker, he knew "only the baptism of John." After hearing him speak, Aquila and Priscilla realized he did not know the gospel or the Lord Jesus Christ personally. Instead of embarrassing him publicly, they approached him and invited him over for fellowship: ". . . they took him unto them." *(Acts 18:26)* In that quiet setting, they won this mighty orator to the Lord. Scripture says they "expounded unto him the way of God more perfectly." Like the Ethiopian eunuch, this man needed someone to guide him and to explain the Scriptures to him. Because of their patience and soul-winning efforts, Apollos was saved and became a mighty preacher for the Lord. Their missionary effort had begun!

Aquila and Priscilla did not worry if their names were great; they lived for others. "If we cannot be great, by God's grace we may be the means of making others great." *(Lockyer)*

Her Fervent Hospitality (Acts 18:3, 11; Rom. 16:3-4; 1 Cor. 16:19)

Can you imagine having company for eighteen months in your home – their clothing to wash, their meals to prepare, their messes to clean up, their schedules to work around? Evidently Priscilla did not look at Paul's visit as a burden or a hardship. Throughout the Scriptures, we see Paul commending her. He commands in 2 Timothy 4:19, "Salute Priscilla and Aquila . . ." What devoted friends they had become. Paul called them his helpers in Christ Jesus, and said they had even "laid down their own necks" for his life. *(Rom. 16:3-4)*

Priscilla's friendship went much further than her fervent hospitality. She was willing even to sacrifice her life for the furtherance of the gospel. How is it with you? Do you consider it a hardship or an inconvenience to open your home, to tell someone about Christ, to share a meal, or to make a phone call?

Though humble tentmakers, Aquila and Priscilla also willingly opened their home to the mighty speaker Apollos, and were not intimidated by his great speaking ability. Because of their boldness, Apollos met Christ.

Not only did Priscilla demonstrate warm hospitality to Paul and Apollos, but she and Aquila are credited for having a church in their own home in Ephesus. *(1 Cor. 16:19)* Did Paul realize they would become church planters for him there? Did he know that his discipleship would reap such great dividends? Would you be willing to open your home two or three times a week for the sake of the gospel? How far does our hospitality really stretch?

Conclusions

Although once again we have a short Scriptural biography, Priscilla's life and testimony leave us with many points to ponder.

She and Aquila are a perfect example of a beautiful and harmonious marital relationship. Elizabeth George wrote, "Like a pair of bookends, they each hold up their end as they serve God's kingdom." We never see Priscilla acting outside of her husband's authority. She used her teaching and leadership ability with him, affecting others for Christ. How is it with you? If you are married, are you working **with** your husband or **against** him? Are you like a bookend, encouraging him? Do you put him down publicly or build him up, recognizing the talents God has given him?

Priscilla possessed great balance in her life. Not only was she a manager of her home, but she also helped with the tentmaking business. She used her warm hospitality to affect others for Christ and boldly presented the gospel, being a great soul-winner. Have you opened your home to anyone lately? Remember, her name meant "ancient, old-fashioned simplicity." That was Priscilla – "down to earth." Keep your hospitality simple – cake, coffee, popcorn, ice cream, or fruit. A warm, caring atmosphere is the important thing, not how much or what you have to eat! Don't be afraid to show hospitality! Romans 12:13 commands it: "Distributing to the necessity of saints; given to hospitality."

Like Sarah, the missionary wife of the Old Testament, Priscilla was flexible! We do not ever hear her murmuring or complaining about all the moves or the extra work they entailed. She looked at each move as another opportunity to be used of the Lord. She had a willing heart and an available spirit.

Priscilla was a virtuous woman who demonstrated great emotional control. She was loyal to her husband, the cause of Christ, and the Apostle Paul. Fear of persecution did not thwart her walk with the Lord. She used the negative events in her life to bring refreshment to others. ". . .Her whole life represented self-sacrifice and a consecration of all her capacities to the cause of Christ." *(Kuyper, p. 103)* Although there is no Scriptural evidence, tradition holds that Priscilla and Aquila were martyred.

What a godly example for us to follow! Are your capacities and abilities consecrated to Christ?

Priscilla's Roles

1. Tentmaker
2. Homemaker
3. Soul-winner
4. Discipler
5. Exhorter
6. Encourager
7. Missionary

Priscilla's Character Traits

1. Loyalty
2. Faithfulness
3. Submission
4. Tactfulness
5. Discretion
6. Flexibility
7. Hospitality

Chapter 10

PHEBE

A Succourer of Many

Facts

Husband:	None known
Children:	None known
Occupation:	None known
Her name means	"Pure or radiant as the moon"

Phebe lived in Cenchrea, an eastern harbor located about eight miles from Corinth. It was in this seaport town that Paul had shaved his head due to a vow and then had departed for Ephesus. It appears that Phebe was a dedicated member of the church in Cenchrea which Paul may have established during his second missionary journey.

Although only two Bible verses are attributed to Phebe, we can glean much from her character through those fifty-some words. From a small biography, we learn much about a big-hearted lady. Let's explore Phebe's character traits which Paul so explicitly described in Romans 16:1-2.

The Saint   (Rom. 16:1)

Paul describes Phebe as "our sister" in Romans 16:1, depicting her as a born-again believer. We are not given the time or place of her conversion, but her fruitful life bore evidence of a close, personal walk with the Lord. She was a living epistle of Matthew 7:17: "Even so every good tree bringeth forth good fruit," and Matthew 12:33, " . . . for the tree is known by his fruit." Phebe was known by her fruitful life.

Romans 16:1 uses the word, "commends," in Paul's introduction of her. Commend means "to approve, to stand with, or to introduce favorably." *(Zodhiates)* Webster also defines the term, "commend" as "to entrust for care or preservation, to recommend as worthy of confidence or notice." Paul held the godly saint Phebe in high regard and entrusted her with a very important mission.

Because Phebe herself had demonstrated hospitality to so many others, Paul instructs the Roman believers "to receive her in the Lord, as becometh saints . . ." *(Rom. 16:2)*

Let's accompany Phebe on her mission to Rome.

The Servant (Rom. 16:1-2)

Most scholars believe that Phebe delivered Paul's Roman epistle to the church in Rome. If so, she would have traveled more than 600 miles, most probably by foot to do so. Perhaps she took a small ferry or boat across the Mediterranean Sea at some spot. It was highly unusual in Bible times for a lady to travel so far from her home. What an adventure for her it was, affording many discomforts along the way.

> 'Phoebe had traveled over land and over water. Her feet had blistered from her endless walks over rocky, mountainous roads. Her nerves had been tested when she crossed from Macedonia to Italy in a creaky little ship. But under all these circumstances she always remained conscious of her task. She had to deliver Paul's letter to the Christians in Rome undamaged.' *(Karssen, vol. 2, p. 227)*

Did someone go with her to encourage her? Did she stop at the various churches along the way for rest and refreshment? Were there prophet's chambers at certain places? Perhaps she was a lady of some means and could afford bed and breakfasts along the way. Whatever the circumstances, we find Phebe accomplishing her goal.

How eagerly the Roman church must have awaited her arrival! They dearly loved the apostle Paul and were desirous of receiving further instruction and teaching from him. They may have had fervent prayer meetings for Phebe and her safety.

Phebe must have been reliable and dependable for Paul to entrust her with such a monumental task. We once again see how important faithful and fruitful women were in Paul's ministry. They upheld his reputation and remained loyal to him.

Phebe may have had other business in Rome also, as Paul instructed the believers there to "assist her in whatsoever business she hath need of you . . ." Perhaps she was like Lydia, Dorcas, or the Proverbs 31 woman with her own business.

Being known as a "servant at Cenchrea," it is likely that people knew they could count on Phebe to get a job done. Who often gets asked to do something in a church? It is the busy people – the people who will put their minds and energies into it, the people who will make themselves ready and available, the people who are reliable, dependable, and "stick to it"—people like Phebe. Are you a person like that? Can you be counted on to keep your word? Are you ready and available? Do your children see you keeping your promises?

Phebe was a prime example of our Lord Jesus Christ in Matthew 20:26-28:

> 'But it shall not be so among you: but whosoever will be
> great among you, let him be your minister; And whosoever
> will be chief among you, let him be your servant: Even as
> the Son of man came not to be ministered unto, but to
> minister, and to give his live a ransom for many.'

Phebe had found the secret to a happy life, that of being a servant. It has been said, "Happiness is like jam. You cannot help getting some on yourself when you spread it to others." Have you found the secret to happiness?

The Succourer　　　　(Rom. 16:2)

Although Phebe may have been a single lady, she had found the perfect antidote for loneliness. Her life was filled with others. Paul affectionately and gratefully describes her as a succourer, "one who stands by in case of need." *(Lockyer, p. 121)* What a graphic picture that word portrays of Phebe! She was always ready to run to the aid of others. Paul said, "for she hath been a succourer of **many**, and of myself also." Perhaps that is why he had entrusted her with the delivering of his Roman epistle. He had watched her in action and was confident of her ability to follow through. He, himself, had benefited from Phebe's care.

Being a need-meeter, Phebe stood in the wings and kept her ears attuned to the wants of others. Upon finding a need, she would quickly and compassionately try to meet that need. She exemplified Galatians 6:10: "As we have therefore opportunity, let us do good unto all men, especially unto them who are of the household of faith." What a gracious and loving person she was—a lady with a big heart! Because she had such a big heart, she may have had to learn balance in her own personal life also. People who give out have to take in, just as Christ had to draw apart in His earthly ministry and find rest. Do you take time for rest and refreshment in your own personal life?

Conclusions

Dear lady, are you a **saint** like Phebe? Do you have a born-again experience with Jesus Christ? Phebe knew that Jesus had come to earth, died on the cross for her sins, and risen again the third day. She knew she was on her way to Heaven. Do you know that you are on your way to Heaven? Have you confessed your sins and asked Jesus Christ to forgive you? Phebe was sure of her home in Heaven.

Because of this fact, she was able to whole-heartedly serve her Lord and her church. Are you a **servant**? Are you teaching your children to serve or to be served? Do they see in you a good example of a servant's heart, a kindness, and a compassion for others? Are you serving in some capacity in your local church? If not, what service would Christ have you do? There is always an area of service in every church for each believer. Paul taught this in 1 Corinthians 12: "Now there are diversities of gifts, but the same Spirit. And there are diversities of operations, but it is the same God which worketh all in all." *(1 Cor. 12:4, 6)* "But now hath God set the members every one of them in the body as it hath pleased him." *(1 Cor. 12:18)* He also said in 1 Corinthians 3:9, "For we are labourers together with God: ye are God's husbandry, ye are God's building." How does God's building (the church) work? "In whom the whole building fitly framed together groweth unto an holy temple in the Lord:" *(Eph. 2:21)* We are to serve the Lord together in a united local body. Though our gifts and talents may differ, when we put them all together, they become a great blessing of harmony unto the Lord.

Are you a **succourer,** a need-meeter? Do you stand by in case of need, quick to run to the aid of others? Phebe's life never held a dull moment. When facing a discouraging day, she did not dwell on her own problems, but reached out unto those around her. Having done that, her problems did not loom as large on her horizon. She did not "give in" to despair and gloom. She was too busy to consider that. She persevered in her service and went the second mile.

Perhaps you are serving whole-heartedly in your Christian life. Maybe you are on the other end of the spectrum. Maybe you do not know how to say, "No." You are afraid of offending or hurting someone. Dear lady, you **cannot** be all things to all people. God has called us as wives and/or mothers to take care of our own families first. However, this is not to be a selfish thing, such as "us four and no more," but a balanced practice. Remember that the Proverbs 31 woman had a balance in her home (see *Women of the Bible, vol. 1, Helpmeets and Homemakers, p. 35*). Yes, she had many responsibilities, yet she still had time for her ministry to others. Let me encourage you with Galatians 6:9: "And let us not be weary in well doing: for in due season we shall reap, if we faint not." Pray and ask the Lord in which ministry He would have you participate. If you have little ones at home, pick one or two areas where your talents may be used and serve the Lord whole-heartedly in those areas! Remember, your family is also a large part of your ministry!

You may ask, "How do I say no?" Perhaps you can say, "No thank you, but I will not be able to do that." Put a final tone in your voice without thinking you have to give a reason or explanation for your refusal. Often our problem is one of comparing our areas of service with everyone else's. We think we do not measure up if we are not doing the same as other ladies. Paul expressly forbade this in 2 Corinthians 10:12: ". . . but they measuring themselves by themselves, and comparing themselves among themselves, are **not** wise." Stop looking at others, and seek God about what **He** would have **you** do! Phebe did not measure or compare. She knew what gifts the Lord had given her, and she knew how and where to use them.

Let your service be the happy part of your life, not a drudgery! Then one day the Lord will say, " . . . Well done, thou good and faithful servant: thou hast been faithful over a few things, I will make thee ruler over many things: enter thou into the joy of thy lord." *(Matt. 25:21)*

Phebe's Roles

1. Servant
2. Succourer
3. Dispatcher
4. Need-meeter
5. Saint

Phebe's Character Traits

1. Reliability
2. Dependability
3. Trustworthiness
4. Kindness
5. Determination
6. Motivation
7. Ambition
8. Hospitality
9. Faithfulness

Sources

Briscoe, Jill. *Women Who Changed Their World.* Wheaton: Victor Books, 1991.

Chappell, Clovis G. *Feminine Faces.* Nashville: Abingdon-Cokesbury Press (Whitmore & Stone), 1942.

Davis Dictionary of the Bible. Nashville: Royal Publishers, Inc., 1973.

Deen, Edith. *All of the Women of the Bible.* New York: Harper and Row Publishers, 1955.

Deen, Edith. *Wisdom From Women in the Bible.* San Francisco: Harper and Row Publishers, Inc., 1978.

Fallows, Samuel. *The Popular & Critical Bible Encyclopedia,* Vol. I, II, and III. Chicago: The Howard-Severance Company, 1907.

George, Elizabeth. *Women Who Loved God.* Eugene, Oregon: Harvest House Publishers, 1999.

Handford, Elizabeth Rice. *Women in the Wilderness.* Chattanooga: Joyful Christian Ministries, 1992.

Handford, Elizabeth Rice. *Women Under the Judges.* Chattanooga: Joyful Christian Ministries, 1993.

Henry, Matthew. *Matthew Henry's Commentary,* Vol. II, V, and VI, Fleming H. Revell Company.

Horton, Robert F. *Women of the Old Testament.* London: Service and Paton, 1899.

Jensen, Mary E. *Bible Women Speak to Us Today.* Minneapolis: Augsburg Publishing House, 1983.

Sources (continued)

Karssen, Gien. *Her Name is Woman*, Books 1 & 2. Colorado Springs: Navpress, 1991.

Kuyper, Abraham. *Women of the New Testament.* Grand Rapids: Zondervan Publishing House, 1934 (renewed 1962).

Lockyer, Herbert. *All the Women of the Bible.* Grand Rapids: Zondervan Publishing House.

Matheson, George. *Portraits of Bible Women.* Grand Rapids: Kregel Publications, 1986.

McAllister, Grace. *God Portrays Women.* Chicago: Moody Press, 1954.

McGee, J. Vernon. *Through the Bible With J. Vernon McGee (Vol. 2 and 4).* Nashville: Thomas Nelson, Inc., 1981.

Morton, H.V. *Women of the Bible.* New York: Dodd, Mead, and Company, 1941.

Nave, Orville J. *Nave's Topical Bible.* McLean, Virginia: MacDonald Publishing Company.

Orr, James. *The International Standard Bible Encyclopedia.* Grand Rapids: Wm. B. Erdman's Publishing Co., 1939, 1956.

Poole, Matthew. *A Commentary on the Holy Bible.* McLean, Virginia: MacDonald Publishing Company.

Price, Eugenia. *God Speaks to Women Today.* Grand Rapids: Zondervan Publishing House, 1964.

Ryrie, Charles Caldwell. *The Ryrie Study Bible.* Chicago: Moody Press, 1978.

Sources (continued)

Spurgeon, Charles H. *Spurgeon's Sermons on New Testament Women (Book One)*. Grand Rapids: Kregel Publications, 1994.

Tenney, Merrill, C. (gen. ed.) *Pictorial Bible Dictionary,* Nashville: The Southwestern Company, 1974.

Unger, Merrill F. *The New Unger's Bible Dictionary*. Chicago: Moody Press, 1988.

Vine, W.E., Unger, Merrill, F., and William White, Jr. *Vine's Expository Dictionary of Biblical Words*. Nashville, Camden, New York: Thomas Nelson Publishers, 1985.

Voss, Carroll. *Women of the Old Testament*. Philadelphia: Women's Missionary Society of the United Lutheran Church in America, 1954.

Webster's Dictionary. Miami: P.S. I. Associates, 1986 ed.

Zodhiates, Spiros, Th.D. *The Complete Word Study New Testament*. Chattanooga: AMG Publishers, 1991.

How to Order

(Give a gift to your friends, Pastor's wife, teacher, relatives, or students and save $ in quantity.)

Additional copies of this book are available by mail.
Use the order form below and send to:

Starr Publications
740 Jefferson Lane
Red Lion PA   17356

Or, order online with credit card: www.Starr-Publications.com

Bookstores—Write and ask for a special discount Bookstore Order Form.

Clip, Complete, and Send with your check or money order

Order Form
Please send me:

Qty.	Title	Cost each	Total
____	*Women of the Bible, Vol. 5 Carnal & Conniving New!* *Available October 25, 2005*	$6.60	$ _____
____	*Women of the Bible, Vol. 4 Powerful & Prestigious*	$6.60	_____
____	*Women of the Bible, Vol. 3 Helpless & Hurting*	6.60	_____
____	*Women of the Bible, Vol. 2 Faithful & Fruitful*	6.60	_____
____	*Women of the Bible, Vol. 1 Helpmeets & Homemakers*	6.60	_____
____	*Dress—The Heart of the Matter*	6.60	_____

Subtotal A (add) **$** _____

Less Discount for Quantity   (circle one)......... - _____

3-6 bks 10%   7-12 15%   13-18 20%   19-45 25%   46-75 33%   76+ 36%

Subtotal B   (subtract) .... **$** _____

Add Shipping & Handling in USA by US Postal Media Mail + _____

1-3 bks $ 2.60   4-6 $ 3.10   7-9 $4   10-12 $5
13-16 $5.40   17-22 $.37 ea.   23-51 $.29 ea.   52+ $.26/bk

Order Total (include check or money order for...) **$** _____

Please send book(s) to:

Your name _____

Mailing Address _____

City, ST, Zip _____

Phone # for questions _____

Send order to: Starr Publications, 740 Jefferson Lane, Red Lion PA, 17356